Believe? Why

*A Rational Road From Secularism
To Observant Judaism*

by

Gam Zokanti

Mazo Publishers

Believe? Why?

A Rational Road From Secularism To Observant Judaism

Gam Zokanti
perckay-GamZ@yahoo.com

ISBN 978-1-95638196-2

Copyright © 2025

Mazo Publishers
Website: www.mazopublishers.com
Email: mazopublishers@gmail.com

54321

All rights reserved. No part of this publication may be translated, reproduced, stored in a retrieval system, or transmitted in any form or by any means, electronic, mechanical, photocopying, recording or otherwise, without prior permission in writing from the publisher.

"To you who would like assurance that you are not crazy"

Table of Contents

Preface	6
Introduction	8
Confronting The Profound Questions	11
What Is The Meaning Of "God"?	15
Why Care if God Exists?	19
Rationality Roadmap	31
The Evidence	47
The Source of Moral Authority	63
Coincidences ... Or What?	98
Conclusion	111
Appendix-1	112
Appendix-2	129
Appendix-3	135

Preface

As I write this, Israel is in the midst of an existential crisis after the recent invasion by Hamas resulting in the worst horrific atrocities inflicted upon Jews since the Holocaust. Beyond this, Israel is faced with military threats from Hezbollah, in the north, and its sponsor Iran. This has led to a controversy within the Israeli public as to whether military age yeshiva students should continue to be exempt from conscription into military service. After all, these people receive the same benefit of protection by the Israeli military as all other Israelis, plus their schools typically receive subsidies from the government. "Common Sense" would indicate that their participation in the military is necessary to maximize the strength of the military. So, the question is, *why should yeshiva students continue to have this exemption?*

First, Common Sense, unfortunately, does not always lead one to the Truth. For example, if you drop a heavy metal ball and a light wooden ball from some height at the same time, Common Sense might tell you that the heavy ball would reach the ground first, but the Truth is, both will reach the ground at the same time. You can try this for yourself. (Note, the lighter object must not be subject to air resistance, such as a feather.)

Likewise, Common Sense, here, does not lead to the Truth, which is, as is already known by the religious community, that Torah study and practice are essential foundations for the existence of the Jewish people, that these activities are, and always have been, responsible for the continuation of the existence of the Nation of Israel, as a consequence of the relationship between God and the Jewish People as expounded in Torah.

So the question becomes, *how can we transmit this Truth to the secular segment of the Israeli public in a way that they might find acceptable and convincing?* I used to be a secular Jew; I would have had that same attitude toward yeshiva students, that they, too, should be subject to the draft like everyone else. But, as I show below, I went through an analysis process on the question of the existence of God consistent with the desire to have a *rational basis* for examining the question, *not based on just taking it on "faith"*. For a hint, this process has to do with getting at the Truth through a rational process that can have critical effects on people's lives, as in court trials.

This work is directed toward secular people who are open-minded enough to consider the possibility that their secular views might just legitimately be subject to scrutiny. Then, as a result of that scrutiny, there might come possible understanding, if not total acceptance, of the value of preserving Torah learning in the yeshivot. For someone who is absolutely convinced that God cannot exist and that religion is nothing more than superstition and foolishness, this work will be a waste of his time, and mine.

Introduction

This essay was originally conceived as an outline for a class that I wanted to give. I have attended many such classes as part of Torah learning and learning about the world of Judaism and Jewry in general. I wanted to give this class to help out those Jews who, like me, were raised without substantial Jewish learning and who were searching for the Truth about God and Judaism on a rational basis, without dependence on pure faith. Perhaps someday, with God's help, I may yet get to present this information in that class format.

In this discussion, by "faith", I mean unquestioning belief and trust in a proposition asserted without evidence or verification, rather than its other common definition, loyalty to, and/or reliance on, a principle or person. I don't have any problem with that second definition

Please do not be offended by my writing "God" rather than "G-d" or "Hashem" (Heb.: "The Name") as is customary among many Orthodox Jews. The way I learned it, we must avoid writing any of God's actual names so as to avoid the possibility of desecrating them. But God's actual names are Hebrew names, and "God" is an English name, hence, as I have read it, it is not really a problem to write "God". I am adopting this convention as a matter of familiarity for my intended audience.

This discussion is intended for someone thinking about, "*Why accept the existence of God, why be observant; and on what basis should these beliefs be adopted other than pure faith?*" A member of the audience would presumably be a secular person, not extensively exposed to Jewish education. This was my own situation.

I was born at the end of 1944 in Brooklyn, New York. I grew up on Long Island after the family moved there when I was four years old. Back then, there was a great value

Introduction

held among most Jews to "be American". America was at that time envisioned as a great "Melting Pot" into which all immigrant nationalities would mix and form an alloy which, presumably, would be somehow stronger than its individual constituents. The vast majority of Jews loved this idea, especially after the recent Holocaust in Europe. It held out hope of safety from anti-Semitism such as had never been previously available in the Old Country.

But it came with a price. The admission ticket to the Melting Pot had to be purchased at the cost of a Jew's Jewishness. Oh, you could still call yourself a Jew, but to really be an American, you had to assimilate into the common American culture. That meant, for example, you couldn't keep that kosher diet any more with foods from local markets, restaurants or your neighbor's cookout; you couldn't make a spectacle of yourself with dress in that distinctive modest Jewish manner, particularly men wearing that funny beanie; you had to adopt American style names so that you wouldn't seem to be some kind of foreigner or "greenhorn" immigrant; you had to send your kids to public schools. Most of all, you could no longer follow the rules for how a Jew observes the Sabbath, since they just didn't fit in with everyone else's common customs. You just *had* to drive to anywhere of interest since most of these places were no longer within walking distance in the suburbs. You *had* to watch that TV program that everyone else watched. Perhaps you even had to work on Saturday just to keep up with the Joneses. You could "be American", as long as you weren't too Jewish.

But if you weren't going to be so Jewish, then there was no point in learning how to be that Jewish. There was no need to learn how to "keep kosher" if you weren't going to keep kosher. There was no need to support a Jewish school if you were going to send your kids to public school. There was no need to learn how to observe the Sabbath if you weren't going to keep the Sabbath. Oh, it was OK to be able to palaver a

Introduction

few words in Yiddish with your fellow Jew and meet at the Jewish Community Center for swimming and tennis. Bagels and lox were in, but Torah was out. The ultimate result of the lemming-like rush of American Jewry into the Melting Pot was the emergence of generations of Jews who only knew that they identified as Jewish and were expected to marry Jewish spouses and *maybe* attend services just on Rosh Hashanah and Yom Kippur, but virtually nothing of what being Jewish is really about: Torah and God. In my own case, I actually never even attended "Hebrew school", and I didn't have a Bar Mitzvah ceremony. This is where I came from, where I had to climb up from.

Confronting The Profound Questions

I had to start that climb in my early 40's when my own teenage children confronted me with the fact that they had decided to become observant within Orthodox practice. How that came about is a whole 'nother story. But I was faced with the questions, "why are they doing this?", "just what is it they are getting into?", and "why am I *not* doing this?"

Although I have dealt with computer systems virtually all of my adult life, I actually have a bachelor's degree in physics. I have loved science all my life. Through that love of science, I developed strong skepticism toward doctrines that require one to accept various truths that they assert on pure faith. I'll have more to say on this further on, but suffice it to say that if at all I could be made to accept Judaism and its concept of God, I would not do it purely on faith, without the same kind of rational basis I'd have for believing assertions made by science.

It seems to me that aside from heavily assimilated Jews, possibly one who "*was* brought up in it" but is reaching a stage of wanting to re-evaluate life-assumptions, might also find this discussion of interest. Sooner or later, any thinking person ponders the Great Questions: Who am I? How did I come to be? How did the world come to be? What is the purpose of my existence? How can I know that God exists? This discussion will gravitate toward that last question in the list.

I hope you find that this work will challenge you to be as open-minded as you like to think you are. Everyone believes that he is open minded, but when push comes to shove, intellectually, most people usually will dig in their heels and refuse to budge from their own long held beliefs. Here, perhaps, you can relax a bit and think to yourself, "just what if he's right, even though it conflicts with what I've always held?" I think you'll find it a good source of growth.

I also hope to demonstrate that religious people don't necessarily have to rely on being closed-minded. I hope that you see in me an analytical, even skeptical person who approaches the question of the existence of God with an open mind and a spirit of curiosity suitable to a good scientist.

But just why am I giving pure faith such a bum rap? Pure Faith, or its more pejorative appellation Blind Faith, means acceptance of an assertion as true without a factual or logical basis for that acceptance. It means accepting an assertion as true simply because it presents as "self-evident", or because we like the assertion and we want it to be true, or at least because the assertion was made by someone we respect and trust, and whose word we do not wish to challenge.

The reality is, very much of what we accept as fact is actually taken on faith. For example, we take it on faith that when we press the brake pedals in our cars, that they will actually make the cars stop. Just because they've done it in the past is really no guarantee that they will do it at any point from now on. We take it on faith that they will work. All right, you can say, "*The fact that they have reliably worked up until now provides a basis other than pure faith that they will work. There is some faith involved, but their history of reliability goes beyond that.*" Fair enough. How about the belief that our next meal won't be poison? I would say that this is much closer to being a matter of pure faith. We also generally vote for political candidates with the expectation that they will be honest and uncorrupted. How often does that bear out?

The problem is, of course, that those beliefs which are taken purely on faith are always in jeopardy of being false or wrong. Normally, that's OK. We routinely go about our lives holding many beliefs which are taken on faith and are actually false. The way we deal with this phenomenon is typically that for those issues which are more important in our lives, we become skeptical and we seek some kind of verification that the information we are given is actually true. We would like to be able to conduct scientific experiments to be able to verify everything, but obviously, this is not practical. So we do the best we can. Usually this comes down to relying on sources which have shown themselves to be reliable in the past.

When it comes to belief in God, now, well, that *is* an important issue indeed. It affects our whole lifestyle. If we've been atheists or agnostics and have led secular lifestyles all our lives, then it will really take some convincing to change our minds and accept a belief in God. Certainly we don't want to take it on blind faith. But if we don't do that, then what do we do about this issue?

That's what this whole discussion is about. I want to give a view of the thought processes followed by this particular scientific and secular person in becoming observant. I will try very hard to keep the emphasis on a rational and analytic approach. As far as possible, I want to ignore mysticism or emotional approaches.

I would actually like to provide some help for persons now engaged in the kind of searching I myself went through. A primary requirement of this process was to be true and honest with myself. I demanded that I adopt a position founded on scientific, or at least rational thinking. If I would adopt any particular belief about God (one way *or* the other), then it was to be because it reflected what I honestly perceived as Truth, and not because I just *wanted* to believe it.

My approach here will be to provide little on what to think, but much on how to think. I'll tell you what I have thought, but I won't tell you what you should think. That is your business.

Finally, I must point out that I am not a rabbi, not even close. Although over the years, I have gathered a significant body of Torah education, and I have lived in a religious Jewish community, my level of Torah knowledge is nowhere near that of a real rabbi. But, as I mentioned, I do have a background in science and computer analysis which presumably gives me some strength in critical and analytical thinking. Having "been there, done that" myself in holding secular beliefs, I can understand the concerns and philosophical agendas of a secular Truth-seeker.

What Is The Meaning Of "God"?

There's about as basic a question as we can get. If we are going to consider whether or not to believe in God, we'd better have a good idea about just Who or What we are talking about. Here, we are taking the classic Jewish concept of God, the Entity Who, as far as we can understand, among other things, is:

- The Creator of the universe, Who is omnipresent and Whose existence is not constrained by time or space, as we know it.
- Transcendent. Existing in a realm outside of our own space and time; regarded as "incorporeal" by humans.
- Sentient. He has understanding and awareness of Self and others, as we understand it.
- Unitary and Solitary. He is not a combination of multiple components, and He alone is the only true God.
- Intelligent and Omniscient, knowing all there is to know about everything, and able to rationally assess it all.
- Caring for Humanity, desiring and arranging for Good as an ultimate outcome for humanity.
- Purposeful, having created the universe with purposes in mind, full understanding of which is ultimately beyond us.
- Permanent. We are excluding an entity that pops in and out of existence.
- Omnipotent – All-powerful, capable of doing anything He desires to do, such as Creating and managing a

universe. This leads to the classic question, "*Can God create a rock that He cannot lift?*" The problem that this question really brings up, of course, is, if God is All-powerful He should be able to do anything including create a rock that He cannot lift, but if He cannot lift the rock, then He can't be All-Powerful. The problem is that such a concept of "All-powerful" is *ipso facto* self-contradictory. It cannot logically be applied to *any* entity, including God. The Jewish concept of God holds that He can do anything He desires that does not involve such an illogical concept.

That is the God we are talking about. We are not talking about any other concept of God, and specifically we are *not* talking about the Christian concept with its additional ideas of God manifesting Himself on Earth through the form of a man.

Until I reached the point of doing the analysis that we are about to discuss, I held an agnostic view: "*Maybe God exists and maybe He doesn't. I know that historically, it has been well established that it is not possible to prove that God exists or does not exist. I haven't seen anything to supersede that, so I'll just let it go at Maybe.*" This seemed to be a reasonable stance, being nice and intellectually neutral and open-minded.

I once attended a *shiur* (Torah lecture) in which it was pointed out that as a *practical* matter there can be no such thing as an "agnostic lifestyle". You lead your life either according to belief that God exists, and you are going to do what He wants, as best you can or as best you see fit, or you don't. Under the category of "or you don't", either you live as if you believe that God doesn't exist, or you live as if you believe that God does exist, but you do not concern yourself with what God may or may not have specifically commanded. Even if you pick and choose which Commandments you will follow (e.g., you don't murder because you understand the value of not murdering, but you eat pork because you don't see any real moral value to abstaining from it) you are still living a lifestyle that is *influenced* by a belief in God because you are still at least making judgments about His Commandments, even if you are not convinced of His existence.

"*But,*" you might say, "*I don't murder because I personally believe murder is a wrong thing to do, not because it's forbidden by a Bible.*" OK, why do you think it's wrong? You got that idea through exposure to the culture of your society. There are other societies that don't view murder as being wrong, in fact, in some cases, quite the opposite, e.g., "honor killings". Where did your society get the idea that it's wrong? It came from the Bible, either directly, through influence of religious institutions, or indirectly, through the influence of historical leaders who were themselves ultimately influenced by religion. So that idea ultimately does come from a Commandment from God, after all. There just doesn't exist such a thing as a *lifestyle, as opposed to a philosophy*, predicated on "maybe God exists."

As a matter of logic and sense, we might notice that in fact, nothing "maybe exists". Either something exists, or it doesn't. We might not know which is the case for any particular entity, and we might, in principle, never be able to determine which is the case, but independent of our own knowledge of the existence of something, it still either exists, or it doesn't. For example, it may be an absolute physical impossibility for us to observe the matter that has been swallowed up by a stellar black hole, but regardless of that knowledge barrier to us, that matter might nonetheless exist. The absolute impediment we face in observing the matter will not change that.

So, in general, if we say, "something maybe exists", or in particular, "maybe God exists", we are really making a statement about our own knowledge about the object, not a statement about the true existence of the object. God exists or does not exist regardless of what we know about such existence, and *even regardless of what we are capable of knowing about it.*

Finally, we do not think of God as some purely abstract entity like mathematics. His will causes or prevents things from being or happening in the world. If there is a God, then He exists in the same way that anything physical exists, notwithstanding that His environment of existence may be different from ours, e.g., one might presume that the nature of Heaven is different from the nature of the physical universe.

Why Care if God Exists?

If you've bothered to read any of this, then you no doubt already have some idea as to why this question is of interest. For the sake of fully justifying all the effort we're going to put into analyzing the issue of God's existence, I feel it's worthwhile to look at the significance of the issue itself.

Philosophically, this raises the distinction between *Theism* and *Deism*. Theism is the doctrine that holds that God not only created the universe, but that He maintains an active interest and presence in it, and at least from time to time even intervenes in its operations. Deism holds that after God created the universe, he "left town" and has no further interaction with it.

Judaism is a theist religion. It holds that God is there, and that He cares, and that He takes care, etc. Deism is really just a convenience for those who actually want to be atheists, but who still want to pay lip-service to the concept of God to allow for His existence as an explanation for the existence of the universe. In this discussion, when we mention God, we are talking exclusively about the Jewish theist concept of God.

Now that we've nailed all that down, let's look at the importance of the issue of the existence of God. If there is no God, then obviously the very first assertion about Him in the Bible, that He created the universe, would necessarily be false. That would mean that all things in existence are a consequence of a long, if not endless, sequence of random and uncontrolled events, or accidents. Everything that exists other than those things brought into being by the action of Man would exist purely as the result of unintentional happenstance. Even the laws of physics themselves, which govern how all things behave, would also be the results of essentially random interactions of relevant factors.

Well, that might not be so terrible. It would mean that the world exists the way it exists because that's how the cosmic dice rolled. If that's the way it is, then that's the way it is and it would not be an issue of concern regarding how people would lead their daily lives.

But if there is no God, then something else the Bible tells us must also necessarily be false. That is the idea that God gave Commandments to Mankind, and that these Commandments form the basis for all morality and law. In other words, if there is no God then there is no objective or transcendent morality that would otherwise be the product of God's Will.

That means that all morality and ethics, all concepts of right and wrong and good and evil must necessarily be the product of Man's thought and will. This moral law might be the product of the democratic consensus of the population, or it might instead be the fiat of a society's rulers. One way or the other, though, it would be people who decide what's right or wrong. This is the doctrine of *humanism*, meaning that human beings are the ultimate defining source of morality, rather than God (as contained in the doctrine of theism).

There is a distinction made between "secular humanism" and "religious humanism" based on whether the adherent connects his moral principles to belief in God or not. In both cases, the belief is that Man determines morality, not God. The religious humanists would presumably develop their ideas about morality based on what they might believe "God would want". The secular humanists base it on their concept of "rationality".

Unfortunately, the term *humanism* is very easily confused with the term *humanitarianism*, which is the doctrine that people should treat each other with kindness, charity and altruistic motivations. One really has nothing to do with the other. In fact, ironically enough, some of the most humanist of political regimes in history, the French Revolution, and the Soviet Union (both of which were militantly atheistic) were arguably among the least humanitarian. Some humanists like to take advantage of this confusion of terms when they self-righteously make proclamations like, "We subscribe to humanist ideals" as if that were something fine and noble. If you know the difference between humanism and humanitarianism, then you know it may definitely not be.

One of the hallmarks of humanist morality is that it is subject to continual change. This is natural, since as time goes on, people change, and their opinions about what is right and wrong change. Especially in a democratic nation like the USA, society's morality in a very real sense is really nothing more than fashion determined by popular culture.

Perhaps some of you who are interested in this discussion may be relatively young and your memories may not extend back over a long enough period of time for the kinds of changes in societal morality we are talking about here to be noticeable. My memory extends back around 70 years, and I can tell you that the secular and humanist morality prevalent in the USA since the 1950's has indeed undergone some noticeable changes. Here are some examples. Around the middle of the twentieth century:

- Unwed motherhood was outright unacceptable. If an unmarried lady became pregnant, it was regarded as a most shameful transgression. She would often be "sent on vacation" to somewhere secluded so that her pregnant condition would not be seen by members of her family and home community. Once her baby was born, it would virtually always be given away for adoption, otherwise it would be considered an "illegitimate child". Occasionally, the girl/woman would have an abortion, which back then was always illegal except possibly in cases of saving a mother's life or if the pregnancy was a result of rape or incest.

- Abortion solely for the sake of terminating an undesired pregnancy was absolutely universally forbidden. It was illegal everywhere in the USA and in most of the rest of the world as well. Such abortions were always regarded as tantamount to murder.

- Homosexuality was simply unacceptable. The term "gay" at that time meant only "cheerful and happy". People who were recognized as homosexuals were typically ostracized, ridiculed and what we today would characterize as persecuted. They were banned from many kinds of employment, especially jobs involving national security or contact with children. They were stereotypically regarded as belonging only in a few select occupations, such as hairdressers, clothing designers and artists. They typically kept themselves "in the closet" to avoid such discrimination.

- The idea of imagining even the possibility of an organization such as NAMBLA (North American Man Boy Love Association) was utterly unthinkable.

- Likewise unthinkable was the idea of handing out condoms to high school children.

- Promiscuity (what today might be known as "liberated sexuality") held a strong stigma. This was closely linked to the undesirability of unwed pregnancy. Consequently, there was rather a double standard in this regard in that a girl who was promiscuous was scorned, but a boy who was, often was merely winked at and looked upon as "just sowing wild oats".

- Drug use was unacceptable, at least in mainstream society. Everything from marijuana to heroin was completely illegal and there was no question that all such offenses were felonies to receive the severest punishments.

- Divorce had a stigma attached to it. A divorcé was regarded as something of a social or psychological failure, as well as someone who perhaps violated the sanctity of marriage. Divorce rates were far below what they are today, well under 10% as I recall. In most American states, divorce involved a complex legal process, requiring the participants to show "grounds for divorce", such as adultery, domestic violence, non-support, etc. Nevada was an exception to this rule, which made that state a "Mecca for divorce." One of the reasons presidential candidate Adlai Stevenson lost his election bids against Dwight Eisenhower in 1952 and 1956 by large margins was due to the fact that he was a divorcé.

- Public vulgarity and immodesty were socially unacceptable and were vigorously suppressed in the news and entertainment media. The use of "strong language" was unheard of and unacceptable in movies and television. In fact, around 1953 a film called *The Moon Is Blue* created a huge scandal and was actually banned in many places because of a single word which was uttered. That word was "virgin".

All this is not to say that the morality of the mid-twentieth century was uniformly stricter or on some higher level than that of today. For example:

- Smoking was much more acceptable than it is today. Although smoking among young teens was more strongly discouraged at that time than it is today, there were no restrictions against smoking in most public places, and the effects on non-smokers were ignored. Cigarette smoke and ashtrays were pervasive virtually everywhere, especially in restaurants, stores and workplaces. Separate smoking and non-smoking areas were absent in most places with few exceptions, such as in trains and theaters.

- Bigotry was much more acceptable than today. Racial segregation was ensconced in education and many public accommodations. "Restricted" neighborhoods, where Jews and other minorities couldn't be sold property, were common. Interracial marriage was virtually taboo and was actually illegal in some states. Ethnic slurs commonly occurred in private conversations, and even occasionally popped up publicly. Racial and ethnic stereotypes abounded in the entertainment media. Discriminatory want-ads with text such as "Man wanted, 21-35, white Christian ..." were not at all unusual. Accommodations for disabled people, such as wheelchair ramps, were completely absent.

- Drinking and driving was much more tolerated than today. Back then, as long as a drunk driver didn't injure or kill someone, he was actually viewed as nothing more than a comic buffoon. Even when drunk driving resulted in tragedies, courts typically handed down little more than slap on the wrist sentences. Judges who often as not would themselves drink and drive frequently took the attitude "there but for the grace of God go I."

- Spouse and child abuse were given virtually no scrutiny. Only the most egregious cases wherein death resulted ever saw the light of day, which was very rare. Routinely, "wife beating" was regarded as something

that "she had it coming to her."
- Littering was accepted. People thought nothing of jettisoning trash out of their car windows as they drove along. This included not just small gum wrappers, but whole bags of garbage as well. The sides of most non-residential roads were consistently covered by trash. It became a major problem to keep up with it as automobile ownership and usage skyrocketed during the 1950's.

It's instructive to note how this problem was eventually relieved through social engineering. A massive "Don't be a litterbug" ad campaign was mounted in the press, entertainment media and especially in schools. It took a couple of decades until generations who grew up with this ad campaign came of age, but eventually the widespread littering habit was substantially broken, and today the problem is comparatively minimal. This is a good example of how humanist moral values and habits can be changed over time.

What about 40 or 50 years from now? What can we expect in the social landscape as the tides of humanist morality ebb and flow?

- Can we expect that on-demand abortion and euthanasia will become universally accepted, with no one batting an eye when such lives are ended? (We are almost all the way there now.)
- Will NAMBLA become widely accepted? Before you say "never", do you remember the case of the tragic murder in 1996 of a 6-year-old "beauty queen"? She was adorned with cosmetics and dress that made her appear like a miniature 25-year-old woman, with all

of the attendant sexual attractiveness. If you recall, that aspect of the case hardly raised a murmur in our society. If that kind of sexualization of children can be tolerated today, what can we expect tomorrow?

- Will cannibalism become acceptable? Why not? If two consenting adults agree for one of them to pay the other to amputate a limb that the payer will use to make a delicacy, what's wrong with that? If food shortages become sufficiently acute, why not bring *Soylent Green* into reality?
- Will bestiality become acceptable? If the subject lines on the email spam I receive occasionally is any indication, it has already become acceptable at least among some segments of the pornography consuming public.
- Will the private ownership of automobiles become unacceptable? If environmentalists somehow manage to sway public opinion the way that anti-littering and anti-drunk-driving advocates did in the past, it's not farfetched at all.

If moral standards change as people change, what's wrong with that? As mentioned, under that situation, morality becomes nothing more than fashion, responding to popular culture. There's an old saying, "*If you propose to take from Peter to pay Paul, you can count on Paul's support.*" People, in general, will tend to favor their own interests over those of the society in general, particularly if the members of society are not especially bound to each other through religious or other morally oriented institutions. (There will, of course, be humanitarian exceptions.) Especially without an orientation toward a morality based on a Transcendent Source, the overall social morality will tend toward trying to satisfy the material and psychological desires of the people. To see an ultimate result of this, please see **APPENDIX-3**.

Humanism fosters a good deal of what we might call "moral autonomy" if we're charitable, or "moral anarchy" if we're not. Although most people will go along with the prevailing group morality, there will always be some who take the attitude, "*Society's moral values were created by people who were or are no better than me. Why should I hold their values to be superior to my own?*" If there is a prevailing moral value to be tolerant of such thinking, then it's easy to foresee that such attitudes could easily lead to social chaos.

On the other side of that same coin is the attitude of, "*why should I hold my value judgments to be superior to or even as good as anyone else's?*" This leads to attitudes of "*Who am I to judge?*" and "*Judge not lest you be judged*" (which paradoxly enough appears in a bible, albeit not the Jewish one.) This leads to tolerance of behaviors further and further from current social norms and hence, again, eventually to chaos.

One frankly very attractive aspect of humanist morality for many people is that it invariably leads to a great deal of sexual liberty or license. Religious sanctions against promiscuity for both women and men tend to be nullified. Technology and morality shifts in favor of contraception and abortion have been removing the concerns associated with inconvenient pregnancies. Only the presence of fatal or otherwise incurable sexually transmitted diseases such as AIDS and herpes provides any discouragement for this behavior. Presumably technology will eventually overcome even this barrier.

A consequence of this facet of humanist morality is desirability for these people to form intimate relationships in other than traditional husband-wife-children "nuclear families". Recent sociological analyses indicate that such trends lead to instability of society, e.g., with expanding crime, drug abuse, homelessness and declining birthrates. This is strongly associated with children being raised outside of families with healthy influences of both fathers and mothers.

It's clear then, that if God does not exist, then there are profound ramifications for society. Even if the process of the creation of the universe does not have a bearing on our day-to-day lives, the process of the formation of a society's moral value system most assuredly does. Likewise, if God does exist, the same kinds of profound considerations must come to mind.

Even though it might seem rather obvious, let's take a look at just what the ramifications are if God *does* exist.

"*First of all, God created the universe.*" I put that in quotes because interestingly enough, it is a legitimate alternative translation of the Hebrew first verse of the Book of Genesis (which is usually translated as "*In the beginning, God created the heaven[s] and the Earth [the universe]*" [Jewish Pub. Soc. 1917 Translation]). That alternative translation carries profound consequences in itself regarding how the implied principles must be appreciated and understood before the rest of Torah will really be comprehensible, however, I do not propose to delve into that here. It is reasonable to presume, though, that before God created the universe, like anyone who makes anything, He devised a plan according to which it would be built.

Judaism tells us that this plan was Torah, i.e., Torah was the blueprint for the universe. "*Hold on,*" you're thinking, "*isn't Torah the Five Books of Moses, Genesis through Deuteronomy?*" Yes, but it turns out that the term *Torah* has some multiplicity in its meanings. In Hebrew, Torah literally means "instructions" or "law". The "instructions" or "program" according to which God created the universe is called Torah. The physical universe that we observe is hence a manifestation of that

Torah. However, the Five Books of Moses are a manifestation of that Torah as well, and they are also known as Torah. Just to complete the confusion, whenever a yeshiva student talks about "learning Torah", he is talking about study of not only the Five Books of Moses, but also the rest of the Jewish Bible (commonly called the *Old Testament*), and not only that, but also any and all other scriptural literature related to Judaism, such as the Talmud, and moreover, the works of Maimonides and many other giants of Torah scholarship. All of that literature is also regarded as a manifestation of the Torah-Blueprint-Of-The-Universe.

As before, however, the question of real interest is not so much about how God created the universe, but rather whether God is the source of our society's morality, and whether God's Will about that morality is accurately represented in the Torah. After all, at this point there is the possibility that the deists are right and that although God may have created the universe, after that, He did not transmit moral law to Man. Therefore, we want to know if indeed God communicated morality through Torah, and if so, what the implications of that are as far as our responsibilities are concerned.

It is the answers to these questions which will have the profound effect on one's life, especially for those of us who are Jews. For example, in Exodus 20, we find the famous Ten Commandments. We will have to accept the fact that these are *not* the Ten Recommendations, but rather, they are Commandments from God, even though He does not force people to obey them, i.e., allowing for Free Will. We will have to become convinced that this is really so, and that these Commandments apply to us, and not just to the people who were present when they were given. Moreover, we will have to assimilate the fact that these Ten Commandments are not the only Commandments given in Torah, but in actuality, there are 613 in all. Not all of these Commandments apply to every person, e.g., some are only for men, some only for women, some only for a king in Israel, some only for use in the Temple in Jerusalem, etc. On top of all of that, we will need to deal with the relationship between the Commandments (those which apply to each of us as individuals) and Free Will.

Even if you are not Jewish, it turns out that Torah can still be relevant to you. There is a movement known as B'nai Noach (or Bnei Noach, "Children of Noah") consisting of non-Jews who wish to know about principles that Torah has for non-Jews, and to live by them. I recommend you look into this if it applies to you.

In contrast to humanist morality, theist morality, and particularly Jewish theist morality, is based on the Torah, and does not change over time. Interpretations of the Torah based morality can change, for example, interpretations needed to be made regarding the use of electrically actuated objects on the Sabbath, since such objects didn't exist when Torah was given. But the basic moral principles upon which these interpretations were made did not change.

These *are* profound issues indeed. The basic issue is, if God exists and He is the Source of morality, then if we are to be moral people, we have extensive responsibilities in regard to how we behave in our daily lives. And if He is not that Source, then we have to deal with the issue of how to lead moral lives under a humanist system of morality. The resolution of this issue implies that we will choose one of two totally different lifestyles. At a bare minimum, if someone adopts a new belief in the existence of God, if he has any rationality at all, he will now read the Bible in a whole new light. How can we tell which way it is?

Rationality Roadmap

As I said earlier, blind faith is not sufficient. In addition to problems I mentioned previously, there is also the difficulty that it has no limits. In other words, there is no limit on what one may believe about God if one takes belief in God as nothing more than a matter of blind faith. This is grossly insufficient for a rational person. If we are rational, we want to believe only that which is true, and not that which is merely desirable to believe but is otherwise untrue. We will need some intellectual tools for being able to tell the difference. Further, blind faith tends to be an emotional matter. We tend to have blind faith in those ideas that we like and not in those we don't like. This also is unacceptable for rational analysis.

One way of rationally approaching the issue of belief in God, and in choosing the effect this will have on your life, is through a construct known as *Pascal's Wager*. This concept comes from Blaise Pascal, a 17th century French mathematician. The idea is that we consider two possibilities about the existence of God:

A. God exists.

B. God does not exist.

Then we consider two choices for a lifestyle:

1. Live a moral life (consistent with whatever we sincerely believe about how God wants that)

2. Live an immoral, or at least amoral life (taking no cognizance of what God might want)

Now, consider the consequences of the four combinations of these propositions.

A-1. If you live a moral life and God exists, then presumably you might be eligible for a great reward in a possible afterlife, in addition to living a life that keeps your conscience comfortable. You will need to restrain yourself from indulging various physical or emotional urges, but you will have the conviction that it's worth it.

A-2. If you live an immoral or amoral life and God exists, then presumably you might be in jeopardy of great punishment in a possible afterlife, and possibly suffer frustration of your current life's desires by Divine interventions.

B-1. If you live a moral life but there is no God, it may have cost you deprivation of some "worldly" pleasures, but you otherwise have the satisfaction that living a good life is its own reward.

B-2. If you live a life without morality and there is no God, then you might get to enjoy all the otherwise illicit physical pleasures available to you and even commit all manner of crimes and suffer no consequences of Divine punishment, but you might still suffer psychological consequences of leading a "shallow and empty existence" and also face social sanctions.

The result is, if you live a moral life, then at worst you might unnecessarily miss out on some physical pleasures, but at best you stand to receive great rewards in an afterlife. But if you live a life without morality, then at best you will get to enjoy various physical pleasures that you would not otherwise, but at worst, you are in for some industrial strength Divine punishment. So in light of this, the rational choice would be to live the moral life, since that maximizes the probability of a desirable outcome, and minimizes the probability for an undesirable one.

Well, that's rational all right, but it comes with some big problems. First, it's intellectually insincere. We would lead a moral life, but we would be doing it for the wrong reason. We would be doing it because we just wanted to win Pascal's Wager, rather than because we sincerely believed that it was the right thing to do, much less because we actually believed that God exists.

Next, especially in Judaism, there is a Commandment, DEUT. 6:5 "*You shall love the Lord your God with all your heart and with all your soul and with all your might.*" This means that we *do* have to be sincere in our being religious, or, in some sense, "it doesn't count". Finally, it does nothing to answer our questions about whether or not God really exists and gave us His moral law to follow.

So, we're still faced with a question of how to rationally arrive at a belief about God that we can accept as true. Let's take a look at the concept of *belief* and the questions, *Why hold any particular belief?* and *How are beliefs formed?*

Sooner or later, if it hasn't already happened to you, you are going to come into a situation where something you were involved in didn't turn out the way it should have. You will have to account for it to someone, and somewhere in your explanation you will utter the words, "I assumed ...". At that point, the person to whom you are giving the explanation will cut you off with a brusque, "Don't make assumptions!" which will leave you feeling about one millimeter tall. Sound familiar?

The appropriate response to that statement is "Bull feathers!" or perhaps something even stronger. The fact of the matter is, it is *impossible* to function on any level without making some assumptions somewhere. For example, you cannot take a breath without assuming that the air you breathe will contain enough oxygen. You cannot take a step without assuming that the floor will not collapse beneath you.

You cannot utter a word without assuming that you will be heard and understood. And on and on. No, you cannot exist without making assumptions. The trick is to avoid making bad assumptions, not at all a trivial matter.

Assumptions are propositions that we hold to be true without proof or other substantiation; we have no choice but to accept these propositions on "faith". One way of avoiding "bad" assumptions, that is assumptions which we hold now but later turn out not to be true, is to identify what assumptions we are holding in the first place. This is not always as easy as it sounds. We often are quite unaware of assumptions that we are making.

One assumption that I make in this discussion is that we all understand what is meant by *Truth*. Specifically, Truth is objective and constant for all people; there is no such thing as "your truth and my truth", notwithstanding the fact that individuals may have different beliefs about what the Truth actually is. That being the case, I will further assume that we want our beliefs about God to be the Truth, as best we can determine it.

One approach to Truth is through logic. (Without getting into detail, *logic*, in general, is the set of mathematical style rules which determines the overall truth of a statement like "***IF*** this-something, ***THEN*** that-something", based on the *a priori* truth, or lack thereof, of either or both of the two 'somethings') We will believe a statement is true if we can prove it is true through logic. This is the standard method of arriving at Truth in mathematics, but, of course, it doesn't necessarily have to be limited to mathematics. A proof ends with a logical arrival at the statement that we wanted to prove was true.

But where does a proof begin? It must begin with statements that are true. Aside from hypothetical "given" statements held to be contingently true, where do these fundamental true statements come from? Often, they will be the conclusions of other proofs. Obviously, though, this cannot continue indefinitely. Ultimately, all proofs must start with statements which are held to be true *without* prior proof. In mathematics, these statements are called *axioms* and *postulates* (I will not get into the quibble over whether these two words are actually synonyms.) They are what we have been calling assumptions.

All proofs work by starting with a set of assumptions, then applying the rules of logic to arrive at other statements, which are then regarded as "proven" and true. In order for one person to convince another that his proof is valid, it is necessary for both of them to agree to the same set of starting assumptions. In mathematics, this is not a problem because this issue has been worked on for a long time by many people, and over time, agreement has emerged in the field as to the valid and acceptable set of axioms and postulates. Also, practical application of mathematics has generally been successful. E.g., we can use mathematics to design and build a bridge that we can drive a train over, and it doesn't collapse.

One thing about assumptions is that we would like to rely on as few of them as possible. The fewer assumptions we hold, the fewer *wrong* assumptions we are in danger of holding.

Outside of the world of mathematics, the situation is not so neat. It is often difficult even to *identify* what assumptions are being relied upon, much less get people to *agree* to them. Never mind that most people don't know a syllogism from a soliloquy. In practical life though, even if people do agree upon assumptions and they can think logically, proof is usually *not* the way they arrive at propositions that they hold to be true and that they believe.

For example, do you believe that a high fiber diet is good for your health? If so, why? Did you conduct the scientific experiments and clinical trials necessary to prove such a conclusion? Not likely. Rather, you perhaps saw this assertion repeated in a number of news stories claiming that scientists did do the necessary work and that they reached this conclusion. There is an *assumption* we have here that if we are told the same thing by numerous independent and competing news sources, then it is most likely true. That's what happened with the assertion that a high fiber diet is good for health, and that's why you believe it is true. Proof had nothing to do with it, as far as you were directly concerned. The news reports told us that the scientists did their jobs and came up with this result. The scientists presumably were involved with logic and proofs, but you were not.

Or perhaps you were just told by a trusted friend that a high fiber diet is good for your health. At any rate, the fact is, you believe *virtually everything* that you believe because it comes from some trusted source. There are lots of trusted sources that give you information that you believe. It starts with parents, then goes through family, friends, teachers, news media, clergy, multiple independent sources, and on and on. That's how you acquire your beliefs.

Messages that bombard you continually through the common culture provide great influence on your beliefs. It's not that you particularly trust the sources of these messages, but you usually would have no reason especially to distrust these sources of information, and the repetitions of the messages has the psychological effect of seeming like multiple sources of information, even if they really are not.

A prime example of this is that you probably believe that carbon dioxide is the main culprit causing *Climate Change*, or as it was earlier known *Global Warming*. Like most of you, I became aware of the concern about this problem based on reports of the physical impact of what's known as the *Greenhouse Effect*. It's caused by the action of sunlight on certain gases in the atmosphere, known as Greenhouse Gases, including carbon dioxide, methane, ozone and others. The result of this action is that these gases absorb heat from the sun causing the surface of the Earth to be warmer than it would otherwise be, and this is largely responsible for the fact that life can survive and flourish on the planet.

The problem, though, is apparently that this greenhouse effect is now becoming too strong, and over time is expected to cause the overall climate to become too warm and thus cause problems such as glacial ice melting and sea levels rising to inundate coastal areas. And we are told that people's activities that produce carbon dioxide and methane contribute to this, and that we must do something about this before it's too late.

As I thought about this, I figured that if it's even possible for people to do anything about it, then the first thing to do would be to identify which greenhouse gas or gases are most responsible for the greenhouse effect, and then consider what could be done about them.

So the question that immediately came to mind was, "*Which greenhouse gas or gases contribute the most to the greenhouse effect?*" It seemed pretty obvious to me that the answer to this question should guide people as to where they should devote whatever efforts they could muster to mitigate the effect. Based on the common culture "buzz", it seemed like carbon dioxide should have been the answer to that question, but I noticed that it seemed to be only implicitly cited as such. So that prompted me to do my own research.

Using the Internet to research this question, I came up with some results but **DON'T TAKE MY WORD FOR THIS. DO YOUR OWN RESEARCH!**

According to the results I found, the answer to the question is **WATER VAPOR** (a.k.a. humidity); it contributes anywhere from 50% to over 90% of the greenhouse effect.

Carbon dioxide, at most, contributes only 10% to 20% of the greenhouse effect, and methane contributes less. If we could remove all carbon dioxide from the atmosphere, we would have only a marginal effect on global warming. We would just kill off all plant life, and then all animal life that depends on plant life. The obvious source for most of the water vapor that we would need to remove from the atmosphere to really mitigate global warming is *evaporation from the oceans*. What can we imagine should be done about that?

The point here is that endless propaganda messages spread through the common culture can definitely have an effect on people's beliefs, even if those messages which, for example, blame carbon dioxide for the bulk of global warming are actually wrong. Unfortunately most people don't have the time or inclination to verify these messages and consequently, they can have an influence on public policy that they really shouldn't have. E.g., the government might favor or even subsidize the use of hydrogen rather than gasoline as a vehicle fuel because burning gasoline generates carbon dioxide, whereas burning hydrogen does not. But it turns out that burning hydrogen produces water vapor as its combustion product ($2H_2 + O_2 \rightarrow 2H_2O$), thereby *INCREASING* the greenhouse effect and the alleged global warming! We need to be careful about whose messages we trust.

Sometimes that trusted source is yourself. If you found that the brakes in your car have always made it stop before, then you *believe* they will continue to do so. You don't always need repeated experiences to form beliefs. At some point early in your life you put your hand near a flame and quickly formed the belief that it was something you didn't want to do a second time.

The trouble with trusted sources is that you can't always trust them. News reporters often have political agendas that slant their reporting. The scientists aren't always so pristine either. A General Accounting Office study once came to the conclusion that up to 25% of published scientific research papers were based on doctored data. (That gives a whole other meaning to "PhD", doesn't it?)

Even your own perceptions, what you see with your own eyes, may not be worthy of your trust. For example, if you look up into the sky, you see that the sun and the moon are approximately the same size, and that stars are tiny objects only a few thousand feet above us. Yet, we know from science that all these conclusions are false. We look at a block of iron and perceive it as a continuous solid mass. Yet we know from science that it is actually mostly empty space (between atoms and molecules). To that extent, virtually everything we perceive directly is false!

Even if we could be assured of true and accurate perceptions, there's yet another problem. Suppose you want to know what the interior of an orange looks like. If you visualize an orange as analogous to an earth globe, with longitude and latitude lines and the stem representing the rotational axis, and you slice the orange in half through its "equator", you will see perhaps a dozen segments that resemble triangles with the sides near the skin being curved. But if you slice it through the "poles", you will see only two segments that are roughly semicircles. It's the same orange, yet the perception you get about its internal structure varies greatly according to the

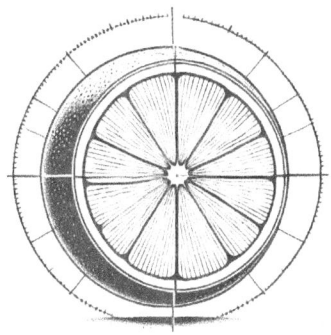

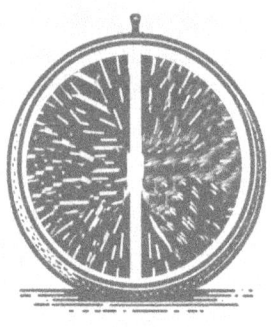

method you use to make your observation.

The point is, we believe all sorts of things based on authority or direct observation, rather than proof, despite the fact that these sources may not actually be as reliable or trustworthy as we would like.

And even if we *could* routinely arrive at our beliefs through logic and proofs, there's still the problem of reliance on false assumptions. This is a lot more likely than you might expect. Here's a classic example.

If you ask virtually any business proprietor, "*Why are you in business?*", the virtual knee jerk response will be, "*To make money.*" It doesn't matter what business he may be in, that's what the response will virtually always be. This is the cast-in-stone assumption as to the main reason people go into business.

Now consider this *true* story: In the early 1970's an article appeared in *ComputerWorld*, a computer industry trade newspaper. It told of a group of gentlemen in Toronto who wished to start up a remote access "timesharing" computer service company. Back then, there were no such things as microcomputers. All commercially available computers were large and very expensive. Machines of the type that they needed cost millions of dollars to buy or many thousands of dollars per month to rent. The men didn't have enough money to acquire any of these systems, but they did have an idea about how to get it.

They decided to produce and distribute a few "adult"

films and acquire the necessary funds that way. It turned out that they made so much money making and selling those films that they dropped the idea of going into the computer business and just continued to produce the films.

The point is, *if you believe that you are in business just to make money, then chances are, you are in the wrong business!* As shown above, you can likely make more money by going into another business, as the gentlemen from Toronto did. So, if you are a business proprietor, just why *are* you really in the business you are in?

Yes, you do have to make money, but your choice of which business to pursue will depend on perhaps many other factors, such as your education and skills, your family background, your ethical standards, your preferences regarding how you like to spend your time and the kinds of people with whom you like to associate, your desire not to get into gunfights with your competitors, etc. But if you don't realize this and you make business decisions predicated on the assumption that the essential reason you are in business is just to make money, then you run a big risk of making some bad decisions, conflicting with the philosophical and motivational foundations of your business. As someone once said, "*I climbed the ladder of success, only to find that it was resting against the wrong wall.*"

The risk of making wrong assumptions isn't *totally* hopeless. There is, at least, sometimes a way of recognizing if an assumption is false. That is, if an assumption can logically lead to a contradiction, then that assumption must be false. In other words, if an assumption you are questioning leads to a conclusion that "X is true", but another assumption that you are *not* questioning leads to a conclusion that "X is false", then you would normally conclude that the (first) assumption in question is false. That, of course, is predicated on the further assumption that that second assumption, the one you weren't questioning, was really the true assumption. The existence of the contradiction is a guarantee that at least one of the assumptions is false, but it doesn't guarantee which one it is.

Generally, to convince ourselves that our beliefs are true, we tend to look for consistency. If a belief that we are questioning is consistent with a sufficient number of other beliefs that we don't question, we generally tend to accept that first belief. This is analogous to accepting information from multiple independent trusted sources. Again, this is no guarantee, but we usually find it's a successful tactic.

So, we are now left with a situation in our quest for the Path to Truth in which we find that there is no guaranteed method for arriving at the Truth, not even proofs! So, what do we do? We do the best that we can, and presumably, we would want to do the best that we can in situations where determining the Truth can have direct and profound effects on people's lives, *in court trials.*

A primary object of a court trial is to reach a verdict. A defendant will be found guilty or not guilty in a criminal trial, or a judgment will be found for either the plaintiff or the defendant in a civil trial. Obviously, the way the verdict goes can have a dramatic effect, particularly on the life of the defendant, but also even on that of the plaintiff or prosecutor. But just what is a verdict? A verdict is a belief. It is a statement of what the court believes about the veracity of the case against the defendant, either criminal or civil.

Likewise, a belief is a kind of verdict. The idea here is that any time you arrive at a belief about anything, in order to get there, you hold a "trial" in your mind, examining and evaluating the evidence for and against the conclusion in question. You are the judge and jury of one, but at the end of the trial, you reach a verdict about what you will believe. That verdict is the belief. One advantage we have over an actual court is that as soon as new evidence comes to light, a new trial can be conducted immediately, and a revised verdict can be reached.

Bear in mind that when I compare the formation of a belief to the arrival at a verdict in a court trial, I am specifically referring to a realistic court trial, not necessarily the kind that we've seen on TV. Trials portrayed on TV have improved in their realism over the way they used to be years ago, during, say, the heyday of the Perry Mason show. If you recall that show, and others of that era, after questioning the witnesses, the brilliant lawyer would point out a spectator and announce that that person, rather than the defendant, was the true guilty party, then give an irrefutable analysis as to why it was so. At that point, the true guilty party would confess, and all accusations against the defendant would be dispelled.

As I say, real-life court trials are not like that. In a real-life trial, both sides present their evidence and their criticisms of their opponents' evidence, and it's not necessarily at all clear cut by the end of that process which way the verdict should go. The court (a judge or judges with or without a jury) may need to systematically analyze the evidence, and this may take days or even weeks. After all is said and done, the court will make its call on the verdict based on probabilities. There will virtually never be a certainty. Based on what it finds is the most probable version of the truth that it can determine, the court will reach its verdict, and that's the best that it can do.

Formation of a belief works the same way. You gather as much information as you can in whatever time frame is available (which may vary from years to fractions of a second), you hold a "trial" in your mind, and you reach a "verdict". That verdict is the resulting belief that is formed by the process.

Belief in God works the same way ... or does it?

One reason a secular person will demur on belief in God has to do with the level of significance of the subject in which the belief will have influence. "*It's fine to form a belief about which brand of corn flakes I should buy by just evaluating probabilities. But embracing a previously unadopted belief in God can have a major impact on how I lead my life. Before I would do that, I want to see proof that God exists; I don't want to rely on guesses.*"

That does sound reasonable. The more significant the issue, the better the basis should be for forming beliefs about it. For the most significant issues, the most stringent basis of all should be sought, i.e., proof. Isn't that the way a rational person leads his life?

Let's examine that question. What are some of the most significant issues in your life, aside from whether to accept belief in God? How about the choice of your home? The choice of your home is virtually right next to the essence of your being. Certainly, it's among the most significant issues of your life, financially, if nothing else. You want your home to be in the best possible situation you can find, so that your life can be secure, you can have access to all the necessities and luxuries of life that you require, your kids can go to the best schools, etc.

Now, before you made your choice for your home, did you *prove* that it is the very best possible choice that could have been made, e.g. through some sort of logical analysis or scientific study? Is it even possible to fashion such a proof? I didn't think so.

How about beliefs you hold in regard to what career you should have, or who should be your spouse? Did you, or can you *prove* that you made the best possible choices on those issues? Of course not. It isn't possible to prove that such choices were optimum. There is never sufficient data available to make such a proof, if by "proof" here, we would mean conducting some sort of scientific experiment. It's simply impractical.

So, what do we do? Again, we gather as much evidence as we can, we hold a trial in our mind, and we reach a verdict, which then becomes our belief on the matter. That's really all we can do. It is simply unrealistic and unreasonable to demand "proof" that "correct" choices were made on such issues.

This is actually all part of the process of being an executive over one's own life. A business executive once told me, "*Any fool can reach a good decision if he has all the necessary facts, but a good executive routinely makes good decisions based on insufficient data.*" **Insufficient data is the normal condition of real life.**

In looking at the question of whether to believe in God, we are in precisely the same situation. Yes, it's among the most significant issues facing our lives, but just as with these other issues, there simply doesn't exist "sufficient data" upon which to perform a definitive analysis, as has been historically established, consequently it's likewise unrealistic and unreasonable to demand "proof", one way or the other. Even if it *were* possible to provide a proof, we would still have to come to grips with the fact that such a proof ultimately rests on the strength of the fundamental assumptions that begin the chain of logic that leads to the proof. And those assumptions, themselves, are inherently not provable and always subject to some doubt.

If we are going to be honest with ourselves, we must admit in light of this that demanding "proof" for the existence of God is really just a mechanism for avoiding facing the issue and hiding behind the unavailability of "sufficient data". Presumably, since you are reading this, you are interested in actually dealing with the issue. Therefore, I hope I have convinced you at this point, at least, that a demand for mathematics-style proof of the existence of God is not reasonable. Rather, like any other major life decision, this issue must be based on probabilities and a verdict must be reached based on a trial in your mind over the evidence.

Now that we've settled that, let's take a look at the evidence.

The Evidence

The first fact that we need to consider for evidence is the observation made early in the twentieth century by Edwin Hubble and others that we live in an expanding universe. In other words, as we look out at objects in the universe, on the scale of interstellar distances, all objects are moving away from each other. Hence, the totality of space occupied by all objects, regardless of what set of objects is selected, is always increasing.

Until this observation was made, it was believed in the scientific world that the universe was static with respect to the way objects, e.g., stars, occupy space, that the way it exists in the present is the way it will always exist, and more importantly, is the way *it has always existed*. This was important because it provided very nice support for the secularist view of creation held by the scientific establishment. In fact, this static universe theory implied that there actually was no single creation event that started the universe. If this was true, then the very first statement in the Book of Genesis could not be true, at least not in any literal sense, and it would be an intellectually defensible position to assert that what the Bible says about God is not true, and even that there would be no reason to believe that God exists.

Not only that, but another major consequence of this theory is that the universe has existed for an infinite amount of time. If that is true, then extremely improbable events, such as the creation of life through the random interaction of molecules, which we will discuss below, no matter how improbable and no matter how much time would be reasonably expected to elapse before it could happen, would always have sufficient time to occur. An infinite amount of time is sufficient time for anything and everything. That being the case, then there would never be a justification for characterizing, say, life or the balance of life supporting conditions on Earth, as miracles. Given enough time, these things could be expected to come into existence by themselves, without any Divine intervention. If we have eternity available, we always are given enough time.

This, of course, was all very convenient for those who wish to hold the atheist view. One could actually say that based on this atheism is a scientific doctrine, and that religion is really nothing more than mythology and superstition.

The discovery of the expanding universe did pose some minor inconvenience for this view. After all, if we look at the expanding universe and imagine running time backwards, it would seem that we should eventually reach a point at some time in the past when the universe would have started out with all possible mass collapsed into a single massive entity. One could suppose that Creation started there.

This gave some slight comfort to believers in the Bible, but not really very much. For one thing, running time backwards to such a point of Creation would require billions of years, not the few thousands of years that one would infer from reading the Bible and "doing the math". Also, under this scenario, the universe starts out containing a large lump of mass, all the mass that is later found in the cosmos, rather than being empty, as is asserted by the Bible (*GEN. 1:2 Now the earth was unformed and **void** ...*).

Further, the scientists observed that if we look at the distant universe and compare it to the nearby universe, we find that the two look essentially the same. Specifically, it does not look like the population density of objects in the distant universe is substantially different from the population density of objects in the nearby universe. In other words, if we look at about a billion cubic light years of nearby space, vs. a similar volume of distant space, we would find about the same number of stars in both.

The Evidence

If the universe had been created by the explosion of a primordial supermass, then a population density disparity somewhere would be expected (i.e., lower population density at greater distances from the center of the original explosion), but it was not found. This prompted the scientists to theorize that a continuous process of creation was going on, that as stellar objects became sufficiently distant from each other, new mass would be spontaneously created in empty space, simply as a property of space itself. This accounted for the uniform population density of objects observed. But more importantly, it preserved a model of the universe devoid of a single starting point. It still allowed for an eternally old universe. The atheists were still happy. At least, they were happy for a while.

Things changed when a new observation came to light in 1965. At that time, the scientists Arno Penzias and Robert Wilson made an observation about background radio waves coming from space. They noticed that there was a uniform pattern of background radio noise in the 3-Kilohertz area of the radio spectrum. This pattern was the same in all directions one looked at in space.

Without going into all the physics involved here, suffice it to say that this observation could not be explained by the existing cosmological models of the time. This could only be explained by the existence of a very special explosion at some fixed point in the past. What was so special about this explosion was that it could not have been some supermass of any finite size that exploded, rather the explosion must have originated with an infinitesimally small point. And not only did this exploding point cause all mass to come into being, but also all energy and all space and time itself.

One might ask, "Time itself came into being? How can that be? What happened before that?" The only way to understand that is that it's like asking "Where is north of the

North Pole?" I.e., we need to think of the Big Bang as being something of a temporal North Pole.

This looked a lot more like Biblical Creation than anything else that had ever been theorized in modern times. There was still the problem that this explosion was billions of years in the past, but at least it was now much more consistent with virtually everything else related in the Book of Genesis.

This Big Bang Theory obviously carries some important implications in relation to the issue at hand here. The primary assertion of this theory relevant to this discussion is that the universe as we know it started at some specific time in the past and the age of the universe is finite and limited. This, in turn, raises the question as to whether there is a sufficient amount of time for life to appear on Earth as a matter of chance.

The theory also seems to indicate that the entire universe we see has existed for only around 14 billion years. Recent analysis appears to indicate that life initially developed relatively early in this universe, possibly within the first 5 billion years. Although science postulates that life arose on its own during this time frame, the bio-chemical engineering inherent in living systems raised the question in my mind as to how likely it was for life to have "evolved" out of non-living material from random "natural forces" within this given time frame.

> To examine this further, I imagine I am the first astronaut to visit, say, Mercury, somewhere that no human has ever visited before. I imagine that as I look around the rocky landscape, I find what appears to be the letter "A" carved in a stone. My conclusion at seeing this would be, "*That's nice, but it's very possibly just a coincidence, that it's the result of purely natural, random phenomena*".

The Evidence

As I explore further, I discover what appears to be a message of about 10 words, in a language that I am able to decipher, engraved in a rock slab. From this I might conclude, "*Knowing that humans have never been here before, this is very highly suggestive that someone else has been here and left this message, **BUT**, it's not entirely impossible that what I see in the rock formation is still just the result of random natural forces and only coincidentally looks like a message I can understand.*"

Yet further, I explore more and encounter a fully functional computer system, made of materials different from that to which I am accustomed for fabrication of computers, yet performing all the necessary steps of input-processing-output that any other computer does, producing information that I can understand, and even fabricating other, similar, computer systems as it goes. From this I conclude, "*It's absurd to think that such systems could have arisen here through the interaction of random unguided forces, no matter how long these forces might have been in play. I must conclude that some intelligent life must have been here before and built these systems and put them here.*" End of imaginary journey.

So what does this have to do with the question at hand? Well, it turns out that we humans have made a somewhat similar journey and made similar discoveries. Only this time, the journey is to the nucleus of the living cell. What we discover is that a system is there composed, among other things, of DNA, RNA, and ribosome molecules, which behave like any computer system we have ever built. I.e., the DNA and RNA molecules act as controlling data "tapes" using a programming language, based on four amino acid "letters", that we can decipher. The ribosome molecules process the data, and the outputs are new amino acids and, hence, proteins. This happens in all living cells, including the most primitive. We are faced with the same situation here as with the third incident in the imaginary journey to Mercury. We find a fully functional computing system in a place where no human could have put it.

But consider this hypothesis: is it possible that natural forces could have come together to create the first instance of that system, and that it just replicated itself from there? The non-living building block molecules from which the DNA-RNA-ribosome system is composed are amino acids. Random interactions of these molecules could conceivably *eventually* create the first DNA-RNA-ribosome system. If the universe were eternally old, as was believed before the Big Bang Theory, then it's reasonable to infer that that is exactly what happened. But, as we know now, it's not eternally old; it's only about 14 billion years old, and indications are that life appeared within the first 5 billion years.

If you're not interested in the details of a mathematical analysis of this hypothesis, you can skip down to the Bottom-Line conclusion in the paragraph starting with "*Considering that the odds of winning the average state lottery jackpot are something like one in ten million ...*"

Otherwise, let's be liberal and assume it might have taken as long as 10 billion years for life to appear, and ignore the estimate that the Earth itself is only about 4.5 billion years old. Just what are the odds that the first living organism based on the DNA-RNA-ribosome system was formed through the random interaction of amino acids, without external intelligent intervention, within the required timeframe? Since we're talking about the first such organism, there are no prior living organisms, hence, no possibility of any evolutionary genetic process whatsoever, therefore the only mechanism for the formation of the organism is random chance interactions of existing molecules.

The Evidence

Of course, one problem that immediately presents itself is that ribosomes need DNA and RNA in order to provide instructions on how to process their data, otherwise none of these components have any functional purpose for existence. So, in order for the first organism to form, both the DNA-RNA and the ribosomes must all have come into existence substantially at the same time, otherwise the other wouldn't have been able to function or sustain itself. We'll ignore this little problem for now.

Let's say that the minimum number of amino acid molecules necessary for a viable DNA chain is only about 1000 (it's actually much higher). There would be 1000! (1000 factorial, i.e., 1000*999*998*...*3*2*1) possible ways for these molecules to be arranged, assuming they form up in a linear array (if they form up in more complex arrays [which, of course, they do in the "double helix"] the number gets much larger). Let's be absurdly generous and assume that any group of 950 molecules in a 1000 molecule chain will yield a functional DNA molecule. That means 950! of these arrangements can produce a working DNA molecule (you'd be lucky if even one such arrangement would work). That would then mean that the probability would be about 1 in a little under 1000^{48} (approximation for 1 in 1000!/950!) or 1 in 10^{144} that a random assembly of 1000 of the right kind of molecules would work.

Although it's sometimes theorized that life originated outside of the Earth, we can consider the probability of life originating on the Earth. Let's assume the surface of the Earth was covered with a "primordial soup" to an average depth of 1 mile, then given the radius of the Earth as 4000 miles, and the total surface area of the Earth is $4*\pi*r^2$ or about $2*10^8$ sq-mi., so the volume of soup would be about $2*10^8$ cu-mi. or about $4*10^{19}$ cu-ft of soup. Let's say that each cu-ft of soup contains about Avagadro's number of molecules ($6*10^{23}$), so the total number of molecules in the whole ocean of soup is

53

The Evidence

about $2*10^{43}$ and let's make the further ridiculously optimistic assumption that all of these molecules are the right ones for the formation of DNA.

Let's now assume that all these molecules interact randomly with each other to form 1000-molecule chains a trillion times per second. Therefore, there would be $2*10^{40}$ chains (i.e., $2*10^{43}$ divided by the length of the chain) times 10^{12} trials per second, or about $2*10^{52}$ trial chains per second. Assume the upper limit for the time that life appeared is 10 billion years, or $3*10^{17}$ seconds. That means that there would have been a total of $6*10^{69}$ trial chains available within 10 billion years. So, under these most optimistic assumptions for generation of the required molecules, the odds of getting a good DNA molecule are $6*10^{69}$ times 1 in 10^{144}, or about $6*10^{(-75)}$. That's a *very* small number. How small?

Considering that the odds of winning the average state lottery jackpot are something like one in ten million, then the odds of DNA having been formed through random interaction of molecules within the first 10 billion years of the life of the Earth are like your odds of buying 10 jackpot-winning state lottery tickets in a row. It's pretty obvious that if someone won just 3 jackpots in a row, the state would shut down the lottery and conduct an investigation as to how that happened. Clearly, buying 10 in a row would be regarded as completely impossible. These odds are so bad, in fact, that belief that life could have come about as a result of random interaction of molecules within the available finite time is a *much bigger act of blind faith* than belief that some external intelligence caused it. If we take cognizance of the problems stated earlier:

- DNA, RNA, and ribosome molecules needing all to come into existence together simultaneously (which alone could render the process impossible)

The Evidence

- the DNA and RNA molecule chains containing many more than 1000 molecules
- the DNA and RNA molecule chains forming non-linear complex structures ("double helix", etc.)
- the difficulty in forming beneficially functional chains out of all the possible chains that could form
- the fact that most available molecules are not applicable to formation of the desired molecules
- the estimate that the Earth is only about 4.5 billion years old, not 10 billion

then other, more rigorous analyses yield *even much worse odds*!

In essence, the prospect of non-living molecules assembling themselves spontaneously into living cells is comparable to spilling ink onto paper and having all the works of Shakespeare come out *on the first try!* I believe any honest evaluation of this phenomenon will drive one to the conclusion that such a system could *not* have come about as the result of random natural forces ("evolution"), and indeed, since all life is based upon this system, there is even nothing else to "evolve from". As with the imaginary journey to Mercury, we have encountered a system, a computer system at that, which shows all the hallmarks of a system that humans might have wanted to build but couldn't have. To me, at least, it is **clearly** the product of a highly intelligent ... *something* ... that came before us. Now, whether that something is God ... well, if not God then what? We will consider this a bit further below.

This is clearly inconvenient for the atheist view. As long as there is an infinite amount of time available, even the most improbable events can be expected eventually to happen. But now that science tells us that the time available for the spontaneous formation of living matter is finite, and indeed far too short for it to have occurred within any reasonable expectation given the laws of physics, chemistry

The Evidence

and probability, that puts the atheist in a bind insofar as this phenomenon is concerned. He must deny that life is an intelligently designed phenomenon, despite the fact that living beings exhibit the characteristics of intelligently designed entities.

At this point, we need to get explicit about what we mean by "characteristics of intelligently designed entities". For clearly, if living beings do indeed exhibit such characteristics, that would provide very strong evidence (although still not conclusive proof) that these living beings came about as the result of the action of some intelligent Designer.

In my view, the characteristics of intelligently designed entities are present in living entities by virtue of both their structure and function.

In the structure of all living entities on planet Earth, we find the system, described above, of DNA-RNA-ribosome interacting to produce, ultimately, all life. Within DNA, we find a coding structure, based on four amino acid molecules, which determines the generation of all aspects of a living creature. We, ourselves, can decode the "messages" being transmitted within the strands of DNA, and infer the correlations between particular parts of the coded message, and individual physiological characteristics determined by these message parts. It's even possible to find instances where DNA messages overlap with each other, i.e., a message will start on one part of a DNA chain, then another will start later on the chain, but the first one would not end before the second started.

Any time an error occurs in these DNA messages, e.g., due to environmental pollution or cosmic rays, the result is a mutation. Some proponents of the Theory of Evolution maintain that the mechanism of the evolution process from one species to another is the buildup over time of successive mutations. The truth, however, is that mutations are *always* destructive; they never result in species gaining any survival advantage, consistent with the fact that they come from *errors* introduced into the normal DNA. There is absolutely no evidence either in the fossil record or in laboratory experimentation that mutations have ever caused, or can cause, any species to metamorphose into another.

The point here is that the DNA-RNA-ribosome system is a data processing system, a computer, more sophisticated than any we are capable of fabricating ourselves (prompting some to want to develop business data processing systems based on DNA), and to expect that such a system could come about as the result of random interactions of molecules, particularly within only 14 billion years, is simply absurd. In order for the system to function as it does, the only reasonable expectation would have to be that it was designed to do so. Otherwise, we would have to expect the fossil record, and indeed, the present living population, to be overwhelmingly littered with examples of trial-and-error failures out of which only a few successful progeny carry forward. We simply do not observe this. Rather we find in the fossil record that species remain unchanged over long periods of time, and various species appear and disappear relatively suddenly in terms of geological time.

This also tends to go against the Theory of Evolution. Suffice it to say that this is a problematic theory, at best. Even Charles Darwin, in his *Origin of Species*, admitted that the theory, as he expounded it, could not account for the development of the eye, since a partially evolved eye, unable to provide actual vision, would not contribute to enhanced survival potential of its owner, a necessary component of the theorized evolutionary development.

We also find that this same DNA-RNA-ribosome system is present even in the most primitive life. We find that this system uniformly fulfills the function of passing structural and functional instructions physically, and even psychologically (i.e., instinctual behavior), from parents to children. This tends to support the idea that the system is purposeful, hence part of a Designer's plan.

Finally, all of this forecloses the possibility that this system is the product of chance. The evident age of the universe is simply too short to have allowed the system to have developed spontaneously by chance, and the clear purposefulness of the system indicates that it is the product of intelligent action. This analysis also leads us to exclude the possibility that life evolved extra-terrestrially, e.g., on comets or asteroids, and came to Earth from there. The time limitation alone confirms this.

This now raises the question of Who or What was that intelligent Designer? Let's not jump to the conclusion that it was God; rather let's consider other possibilities.

Clearly a non-Divine designer of such a system would have had to exist relatively early in the life of the universe. It would have had to have had extremely advanced technology, enabling it to develop the DNA-RNA-ribosome system, or at least to distribute it across the cosmos from its origin to Earth and wherever else it might eventually be found. This is the *Ancient Astronauts* hypothesis.

All right, what about Ancient Astronauts? As mentioned earlier, life seems relatively old, first appearing early, within the first few billion years of the life of the universe. We would need to postulate that ancient astronauts evolved, developed advanced genetic and space travel technology, found a suitable environment (i.e., Earth), and colonized it -- all before the appearance of life on Earth.

Where did they come from? If we want to assume that they evolved from natural processes, then we have the same problem with their development as we do with our own, plus with a much shorter time available with which to work. We might consider that their initial conditions were more conducive to quick evolution than ours, but there is no evidence that such conditions exist anywhere.

Perhaps these ancient astronauts were created from previous more-ancient astronauts(?) We could continue to iterate this process, but each iteration would suffer from an increasing time squeeze. All of these factors lead us to conclude that there is poor evidence for the existence of ancient astronauts as the source of life on Earth.

At this point, the secular observer might make an argument like, "*We've solved scientific mysteries before, eventually we'll also solve this one with a scientific explanation.*" What is the evidence that this will work?

Actually, the only reason to think that it's true is that in *An Introduction To General Systems Thinking*, Gerald Weinberg tells us:

> "*We expect the Future to resemble the Past, because in the Past, the Future **did** resemble the Past.*"

Obviously, this is not a guarantee. What's the problem with that in this situation?

At one time, the universe was thought to be static, infinite, and eternal. Then the Hubble starlight spectrum red shift was discovered, and it was thought that the universe was expanding, but still infinite and eternal. Then the Big Bang was discovered, and the universe was thought to be expanding, finite, and not eternal. Now, the latest theories are giving cosmologists fits because observations of the oldest stars seem to indicate that they are older than the Big Bang itself. Here we have successive theories of the universe bringing *radically* different models of the cosmos from their predecessors. The successive theories do not reduce to the previous theories in *any* domain, *which carries the implication that all of the previous theories had no overall validity in any domains.*

Based on this track record, we can have a reasonable expectation that future theories will only continue to contradict the current theories. The point is, in the face of this, any assumption that we'll eventually find a valid model for the nature of the universe, and any alleged propensity for it to spontaneously form life, is a singularly poor one. *It's nothing more than blind faith in atheism rather than face the current evidence for the existence of a Divine Designer.* The fact is, some scientific mysteries remain vexingly unsolved, and the more they are studied, the worse they get. This is particularly true of cosmology. Recent observations indicate that mysterious entities like "dark energy" and "dark matter" need to be postulated in order for sense to be made of observations of the nature of the universe. No evidence has been found to confirm that these things actually exist. Sometimes, observations prompt radical changes in cosmological theories, e.g., Continuous Creation vs. Big Bang. We might likewise expect that today's theories will eventually be found "wrong".

Indeed, even as I write this, some physicists are suggesting a new cosmological model in which Dark Matter does not exist, but the age of the universe expands to approximately 27 billion years. I wouldn't expect this to be the last word.

If Physics returns to a cosmological model of an Eternal Universe, we might go back to a purely secular view, except the Earth is still not eternal, and the problem of limited time for evolution persists.

At this point, the more we learn, the worse it looks for a naturalist explanation for the origin of life. The most recent research has discredited the original Theory of Evolution based on *survival of the fittest* yielding gradual metamorphosis of one species to another. The most modern versions of the theory postulate a doctrine of "Punctuated Equilibrium", which attempts to bring the theory in line with the findings of long periods of unchanging properties in species actually seen in the fossil record. Again, there is no real evidence of any biological mechanism that supports this idea.

Some biologists concede that life couldn't have originated spontaneously on Earth. But if it originated spontaneously elsewhere in the cosmos, the time limitation problem still exists. I.e., even the total age of the universe is still insufficient for the process to materialize, as detailed above.

Having now ruled out naturalistic explanations for the formation of life, then tentatively at least, we can consider a supernatural explanation, such as that God is the most probable explanation. All of this is essentially known as the *Argument from Design*, i.e., the concept that since life exhibits the characteristics of a designed system, that implies there was a Designer.

There are other arguments for the existence of God, but, to my mind at least, they seem weaker, and I don't propose to delve into them very deeply. One is the First Cause argument which posits that everything is caused by something else, and that logically, this chain cannot be infinite and there must exist some First Cause, which would be God. But that would seem to contradict the primary concept that *everything* has a prior cause, hence, the whole argument is problematic.

There is also the argument from Definition, which says that existence of God is mandated in the definition of the term "God". This impresses me as an interesting logical exercise, but it doesn't really expose any objective truth about God or the universe.

So, for the purposes of the trial I'm conducting in my mind, I'll accept the Argument from Design as strong evidence for the verdict that God does, indeed, exist.

We have covered the creation of life as a consequence of the action of a Divine Designer, what about the creation of

The Evidence

the universe? There are, in fact, indications in nature, aside from the phenomenon of life, that Divine design is operative in the rest of the universe. For example, the nuclei of atoms for all elements other than hydrogen contain numerous protons. All protons carry a positive electronic charge, which would normally cause these particles to repel each other, causing the nuclei to disintegrate. But, in fact, there are other forces present in the nuclei, that are found nowhere else in nature, that overcome these repulsive forces, allowing the nuclei to remain intact.

Likewise, the sun and stars derive their energy through the process of nuclear fusion, the same process that makes the hydrogen bomb work. Yet, instead of exploding immediately, they stay together for millions or billions of years due to gravitational and perhaps other forces. All such things also suggest the hidden hand of a Designer, but just the evidence of a Designer for life seems convincing enough.

The Source of Moral Authority

Convincing enough of what? Even if we are convinced that God created life and/or universe, that still leaves the question of whether deism is correct, or if theism is the truth and the existence of God implies that He gave Mankind moral guidance.

Judaism asserts that this Divine moral guidance comes from something called Torah. Earlier in this essay, we covered the various contexts in which the term *Torah* is used. Here, we will use the term to refer to the Pentateuch, the Five Books of Moses: Genesis, Exodus, Leviticus, Numbers, and Deuteronomy.

Judaism asserts not only that this combined document provides God's moral guidance, but that the entire five book document, itself, was authored, word by word, by God Himself Who dictated, as it were, the text to Moses, who then wrote it down to be accessible to the rest of Mankind. This is definitely distinct from humanist belief, which holds that people wrote the Torah. Now, in this context, the term "Judaism" refers specifically to what's known as "Orthodox Judaism", excluding "Reform" and "Conservative" streams of Judaism. In those two streams, the belief is that Torah was "Divinely Inspired" (whatever that means), but otherwise authored by people, not God. These humanistic streams did not exist before the early 18th century; how they came about is beyond the scope of this discussion.

At any rate, it's actually a source of confusion to refer to Reform and Conservative streams as "Judaism", since their fundamental beliefs are so different from the original Orthodox stream, despite their adherence, to one degree or another, to various traditional ritual observances, and the fact that most of their adherents might satisfy Torah-based definitions of who is properly identified as Jewish. However, since the Orthodox Jews never got a copyright on the term *Judaism*, we are now stuck with this confusion.

If Torah does have Divine authorship, then clearly it would be the ideal source of information as to what God wants people to know for moral guidance, and it represents guidance from an unimaginably great Source of wisdom, great enough to have been the Designer of life and the universe. This implies that it behooves us humans to take very seriously the guidance contained therein and conduct our lives accordingly. This now leads to the question of the Divine origin of Torah.

If Torah is not Divinely authored, then, at best, its information is the product of people's thinking, profound though it may be. At worst, it's just a collection of fables, perhaps suitable for the guidance of children.

Now, if this assertion of Divine authorship of Torah is false, then the Torah must have been authored by people, and it must be impossible that any information contained therein could be anything other than the product of the thinking and experience of human beings. Given the minimum known age of the Torah text, at least 2500 years, it would then have to be the product of what we today would call "ancient people", i.e., not "technologically advanced" as we understand the term.

If, therefore, one can find in Torah information that clearly could *not* be the product of such people, i.e., would be patently beyond the ability of such people to produce, then that would tend to support the original assertion that Torah was authored by God, rather than Man. At least it would indicate that Torah was authored by some entity other than Man, and you might then have the problem of coming up with a reasonable alternative for this entity other than Man or God. That gets back into the "Ancient Astronauts" problem seen previously.

The Source of Moral Authority

So the question now becomes: "*Can we find information in Torah that is inconsistent with such information having possibly been written by people some 2500 years ago?*" For me, the answer appears to be, "very likely, yes."

Some examples:

- The creation scenario in Genesis is remarkably consistent with modern knowledge of relativity and genetics. (Please see **APPENDIX-1**.) This is most unexpected for any human writers of 2500 years ago or more, and is, as far as I know, unique to Torah.
- The law of "*Shmitah*" is totally inconsistent with human authorship:

> *LEV. 25:1 And the Lord spake unto Moses in mount Sinai, saying, 2 Speak unto the children of Israel, and say unto them,* ***When ye come into the land which I give you, then shall the land keep a sabbath unto the Lord.*** *3 Six years thou shalt sow thy field, and six years thou shalt prune thy vineyard, and gather in the fruit thereof;* ***4 But in the seventh year shall be a sabbath of rest unto the land, a sabbath for the Lord: thou shalt neither sow thy field, nor prune thy vineyard. 5 That which groweth of its own accord of thy harvest thou shalt not reap, neither gather the grapes of thy vine undressed: for it is a year of rest unto the land.*** *... 8 And thou shalt number seven sabbaths of years unto thee, seven times seven years; and the space of the seven sabbaths of years shall be unto thee forty and nine years. ... 10 And ye shall hallow the fiftieth year, and proclaim liberty ...* ***11 A jubilee shall that fiftieth year be unto you: ye shall not sow, neither reap that which groweth of itself in it, nor gather the grapes in it of thy vine undressed.*** *12 For it is the jubilee; it shall be holy unto you:* ***ye shall eat the increase thereof out of the field.***

... 20 And if ye shall say, What shall we eat the seventh year? behold, we shall not sow, nor gather in our increase: 21 Then I will command my blessing upon you in the sixth year, and it shall bring forth fruit for three years. 22 And ye shall sow the eighth year, and eat yet of old fruit until the ninth year; until her fruits come in ye shall eat of the old store.

No leaders of human societies would ever, or did ever, construct rules mandating leaving all farmlands within their sovereign control fallow for a full year. I.e., this law mandates letting all farms in the Land of Israel lie fallow every 7th year and every 50th year and requires dependence on God to supply bumper crops in the years immediately *preceding* the fallow years. And since everyone entered the Land at the same time, everyone observed these sabbatical years jointly with each other. Note: in the 49th and 50th years, all of the farmlands are to be left fallow for *two years in succession!* (Although in the 50th year, they could eat whatever grew by itself.)

If men invented this law, they would be exposing themselves to immense risks of loss of credibility, not to mention economic chaos, if their postulated "Will of God" would not back the law up with the expected bumper crops at the "right" times. Of critical importance is the fact that these required times are the *wrong* times, according to the most elementary knowledge of agriculture, which indicates that the bumper crops would come *after* the fallow years, not before. If men wrote Torah, why on Earth would they include this law?

- The laws requiring all males to go to Jerusalem 3 times a year, leaving the rest of the country vulnerable to hostile neighbors, is inconsistent with human authorship:

    EXO. 23:17 *Three times in the year all thy males shall*

appear before the Lord GOD.

DEUT. 16:16 *Three times in a year shall all thy males appear before the LORD thy God in the place which He shall choose; on the feast of unleavened bread, and on the feast of weeks [Shavuot], and on the feast of tabernacles [Sukkot]; and they shall not appear before the LORD empty*

I.e., back then, as now, Israel was located in a bad neighborhood, with enemies all around. The laws cited require all males to go to Jerusalem (*the place which He shall choose*) three times each year to offer sacrifices, leaving all the other cities and towns in the country defenseless while that was being done. Yet it was done, and the defense of the country never suffered for it, despite the fact that it was done for centuries, and the rulers of the neighboring countries knew it was being done. It is inconceivable that if people wrote Torah, that they would have put such a law into it, given the kind of neighborhood that has surrounded Israel.

- Predictions in Deuteronomy 28 regarding consequences of disregard of the Law and resultant destruction of the Jewish state (which predictions, no one contests, were written well before the destruction of the Second Temple) pose many unusual or unlikely *a-priori* scenarios for such destruction. E.g., it is predicted that the land would be utterly destroyed, cities laid waste, agriculture destroyed, and population completely removed from the land. Conquerors of the era in which those predictions were supposedly written by men, didn't do business that way -- it made no logistic or economic sense, since conquering armies, not having modern-style long supply lines, depended on the produce and labor of people of the lands they conquered. Yet, the prediction is exactly what happened. Also, it was predicted that Israel would be conquered by a people whose language the Jews wouldn't understand and that some of the people would be brought back to Egypt in ships. The most likely people to bring the Jews back to Egypt in ships would have been Egyptians, and the Jews *did* understand their language. So the Bible predicted something quite unlikely. In fact, the Romans conquered Israel, speaking Latin, a language the Jews didn't (at first) understand, and they did happen to deport many of the Jews to Egypt with ships.

E.g., *DEUT. 28:15 But it shall come to pass, if thou wilt not hearken unto the voice of the LORD thy God, to observe to do all His commandments and His statutes which I command thee this day; that all these curses shall come upon thee, and overtake thee. ... :20 The LORD will send upon thee cursing, discomfiture, and rebuke, in all that thou puttest thy hand unto to do, until thou be destroyed, and until thou perish quickly; because of the evil of thy doings, whereby thou hast forsaken Me. ....:48 therefore shalt thou serve thine enemy whom the LORD shall send against thee, in hunger, and in thirst, and in nakedness, and in want of all things; and he shall put a yoke of iron upon thy neck, until he have destroyed thee. :49 The LORD will bring a nation against thee from far, from the end of the earth, as the vulture swoopeth down; a nation whose tongue thou shalt not understand; :50 a nation of fierce countenance, that shall not regard the person of the old, nor show favor to the young. :51 **And he shall eat the fruit of thy cattle, and the fruit of thy ground, until thou be destroyed; that also shall not leave thee corn** [i.e., grain, not maize], **wine, or oil, the increase of thy kine, or the young of thy flock, until he have caused thee to perish. :52 And he shall besiege thee in all thy gates, until thy high and fortified walls come down, wherein thou didst trust, throughout all thy land; and he shall besiege thee in all thy* *gates throughout all thy land, which the LORD thy God hath given thee. :53 And thou shalt eat the fruit of thine own body, the flesh of thy sons and of thy daughters whom the LORD thy God hath given thee; in the siege and in the straitness, wherewith thine enemies shall straiten thee ... :62 And ye shall be left few in number, whereas ye were as the stars of heaven for multitude; because thou didst not hearken unto the voice of the LORD thy God. :63 And it shall come to pass, that as the LORD rejoiced over you to do you good, and to multiply you; so the LORD will rejoice over you to cause you to perish, and to destroy you;* **and ye shall be plucked from off the land whither thou goest in to possess it. :64 And the LORD shall scatter thee among all peoples, from the one end of the earth even unto the other end of the earth; and there thou shalt serve other gods, which thou hast not known, thou nor thy fathers, even wood and stone.** *:65 And among these nations shalt thou have no repose, and there shall be no rest for the sole of thy foot; but the LORD shall give thee there a trembling heart, and failing of eyes, and languishing of soul. :66 And thy life shall hang in doubt before thee; and thou shalt fear night and day, and shalt have no assurance of thy life. :67 In the morning thou shalt say: 'Would it were even!' and at even thou shalt say: 'Would it were morning!' for the fear of thy heart which thou shalt fear, and for the sight of thine eyes which thou shalt see.* **:68 And the LORD shall bring thee back into Egypt in ships, by the way whereof I said unto thee: 'Thou shalt see it no more again';** *and there ye shall sell yourselves unto your enemies for bondmen and for bondwoman, and no man shall buy you.*

- There appear to be hidden messages ("The Torah Codes") imbedded in the Hebrew text of Torah (formed by skipping fixed numbers of letters and creating words from the resultant letters included between the skipped segments) which not only would have been impossible for the authors to have imbedded the way it was done without the aid of computers, but some of these messages predict events (specifically the names and dates of death of famous rabbis who lived long after Torah was written), knowledge of which simply would not have been available to human authors of the time.

These last two items are inconsistent with the Ancient Astronauts hypothesis, as well. I.e., in order for these ancient astronauts to have authored Torah, they would have had to be able to see the future with complete accuracy or have been time travelers, or been capable of controlling events in complete detail from behind the scenes. Therefore, if you want to postulate their existence, you will be creating for yourself entities that are virtually indistinguishable from God in terms of their nature and their "provability".

There's also evidence inherent in the nature of the transmission itself of Torah down through the generations. This gets into a complex argument that's discussed in a book called *The Kuzari* by Rabbi Yehuda HaLevy, written several hundred years ago (12th century).

The argument goes something like this: It's possible, even easy, to get people to believe all kinds of false information. Persuasive storytellers and charismatic leaders do it all the time. If you think about it, though, you might notice that it's really not possible to successfully spread a lie to assert that a major damaging earthquake occurred if, in fact, it didn't. For example, if I tell you the truth and say, "*A major earthquake destroyed most of San Francisco in 1906,*" you will believe it, not because I'm such a persuasive *raconteur*, but because in our society there is ample corroborating information readily available to you that confirms my assertion, so much so that it is common knowledge.

But if I tell you, "*A major earthquake destroyed most of Boston in 1755,*" you would not believe it. That's because other than my assertion, you will be able to find no evidence or testimony to corroborate it, and (*here's the important part*) FOR SUCH AN EVENT, YOU **SHOULD** BE ABLE TO FIND WIDESPREAD CORROBORATION. You should be able to find it because the event would have had widespread impact on a large segment of society (if not the entire society), both in the area and outside, such that it would have been noteworthy, it would have been recorded, and it would have become part of the culture of the society to know about it. I.e., the "Boston Earthquake" would be common knowledge in American society, just as is the San Francisco Earthquake.

Bear in mind that in order to be "successful" in telling a lie (i.e., getting the audience to believe the lie), the liar needs to have two things going for him:

1. He must be convincing. He must be able to tell his lie in such a way that those who hear it will have every reason to believe it and no reason not to believe it.

2. The subject being lied about is something the listener cannot verify for himself, or at least, the listener would have to go to some substantial inconvenience to verify. The subject must *not* be something that the listener can readily verify for himself and thereby immediately discover the falsity of the liar's assertion.

What's so special about an earthquake that makes it so hard to successfully lie about? Why is it that I might be able to get away with lying to a substantial number of people about seeing space aliens step out of a UFO, but I couldn't get away with lying about the occurrence of a major earthquake? It's because such an earthquake is a *very special kind of event* that is **extremely dramatic, and traumatically attention-demanding,** *and it occurs before the **entire population** of a society*.

In a series of Torah lectures at Ohr Somayach Yeshiva, Rabbi Dovid Gottlieb explains that it is that characteristic that makes it impossible to fabricate, as shown above according to the second requirement for a successful liar. I.e., in a situation like this, the prospective liar would be telling a lie about an event that everyone had witnessed for himself, since the event drew everyone's attention to itself, and the witnesses therefore would know the truth, having witnessed it for themselves. If the liar would attempt to assert his lie after the fact, that would still fail, since the nature of the event is such that the event would have to be common knowledge to all in the society, and any lie would either contradict this common knowledge, or conflict with the fact that such common knowledge should exist, but doesn't.

Very few kinds of events are like this, hence all the other kinds of events, which are not like it, are not subject to the same kind of immunity against falsification as this. In other words, it is much easier to succeed in falsely making assertions about such things as divine revelations to an individual or small group of people, because there is no claim that they occurred before an entire population, or even that they were necessarily dramatic or attention-demanding.

We can generalize the operative concept to say, *one cannot successfully falsely assert that an **extremely dramatic, traumatically attention-demanding event** occurred before the **entire population** of a society*. ("Successfully" here means that the teller convinces the *vast majority* of listeners that the assertion is true, and *it becomes part of the culture of the listeners*.) This is because such a false assertion would conflict with the existing lack of corroborating evidence for the assertion.

Now, recasting the principle in If-Then form, it says: *If an assertion about an **extremely dramatic traumatically attention-demanding event** occurring before the **entire population** of a* *society is false, then the assertion will not (generally, widely) be believed.* Why this recasting? Well, if you recall in high school geometry or logic class, you can have an If-Then proposition, say "If A, then B". There are then three other derivatives of this proposition, viz:

Proposition: If A, then B
Converse: If B, then A
Inverse: If not-A, then not-B
Contrapositive: If not-B, then not-A.

Example:

Proposition: If it is raining, then the sky is cloudy. (Let's assume this proposition is true.)

Converse: If the sky is cloudy, then it is raining. (This might be false, the sky might be cloudy without rain.)

Inverse: If it is not raining, then the sky is not cloudy. (Also possibly false, just as with the Converse)

Contrapositive: If the sky is not cloudy, then it is not raining. (This would have to be true.)

Logical analysis tells us that if the Proposition is true, then the truth of the Converse and Inverse are not determined given the original proposition alone, but the Contrapositive *will* be true. In fact, *a Proposition and its Contrapositive are logically equivalent*, i.e., they will be either both true or both false (together).

Back to our case:

A = "assertion [*about an* **extremely dramatic traumatically attention-demanding event** *occurring before the* **entire population** *of a society*] is false"

B = "assertion [*about an **extremely dramatic traumatically attention-demanding event** occurring before the **entire population of a society***] will not be believed".

OK, the contrapositive of our principle will now be: *If an assertion about an **extremely dramatic traumatically attention-demanding event** occurring before the **entire population** of a society **is** (generally, widely) believed (in that society), **then the assertion is true**.* This is a rather astounding result! It says, for example, that if there is a widespread belief in our society that an earthquake destroyed San Francisco in 1906, then that widespread belief is, *in itself, prima facie* evidence that the event actually took place. The reason is, if the event didn't take place, no such widespread belief could have arisen. *The crux of this argument centers around the requirement that the event being asserted* is an **extremely dramatic, traumatically attention-demanding occurrence happening before the *entire* population of a society**, such as a major earthquake.

There are few such events about which this discussion would be relevant. They would normally be natural disasters. In other words, if ***EVERYONE*** in a society believes that a miraculous or highly unusual **extremely dramatic, traumatically attention-demanding** event ***PUBLICLY*** took place before the ***ENTIRE*** population of that society, then that's *prima facie* evidence that the event actually took place. This is a variant of Abraham Lincoln's "*You can't fool all the people all the time*" aphorism.

A further implication of this principle is that *if this specific type of assertion is widely believed about an event in the past and no other evidence of this event exists in the present, then the existence of the belief is, in itself, an indication that the corroborating evidence at one time **did** exist.* Again, this is necessary because without that corroborating evidence, the belief could not have arisen and become widely accepted. This is a very powerful principle for historical analysis. It allows us to infer that a certain historical event actually did occur despite lack of historical documentation that might otherwise normally be required in such cases, as long as it fulfills the proper requirements:

- The event is a miraculous or highly unusual **extremely dramatic, traumatically attention-demanding** occurrence.
- The event took place *PUBLICLY*.
- The event took place before the *ENTIRE* population of the society in question.
- It is possible at least to identify a point in the past, if not at present, where the entire population of the society believed that the event took place.

Again, these criteria are *very* restrictive. For example, this does *NOT* apply to "Everyone knows" statements in general, such as "*Everyone knows the Earth is flat and you'll fall off the edge*," which, at one time, most everyone in Western society might have believed. There was no alleged *UNIVERSAL PUBLIC* witness of any **extremely dramatic, traumatically attention-demanding event** involved in this type of assertion. In fact, this argument doesn't apply to most propositions that are widely believed. This is because very few things about which we hold beliefs involve any **extremely dramatic, traumatically attention-demanding occurrence happening before the *entire* population of a society.**

Normally, natural disasters would be the only kinds of events to which this analysis would apply. There is, however, one historical event other than a natural disaster to which this analysis is also relevant. This was when God came down on Mt. Sinai and appeared before the entire nation of Israel to give the Ten Commandments. Here we have an assertion about an **extremely dramatic traumatically attention-**

demanding event (See Exo. 19-20) **occurring before the entire population** of the society of the nation of Israel, which assertion, historically, until only early in the 19th century, was accepted as Truth by the entire society of the Jewish People. According to the logical principle, this means that the belief, in itself, is good *evidence* that the event actually did happen. If the revelation at Sinai didn't really happen, there is no way the entire society could have come to accept it, especially the Jews, who have always been noted culturally for being "stiff necked" and skeptical. Moreover, if it didn't happen anyone who might have considered asserting it would have known that it is the kind of falsehood that no one would believe, because it would simply contradict well established common knowledge of the listeners.

This was a dramatic miraculous event, observed by the entire population of the Israelites, and, as importantly, believed by the entire Jewish population up until relatively recent times. All the conditions necessary are present for us to conclude that it actually did happen. Otherwise, we would have to believe that the entire nation of Israel conspired on the spot to adopt this supposedly false story encompassing the entire nation, or that later generations formed a conspiracy for the same purpose. The entire edifice of Judaism rests on the veracity of the proposition that this Revelation actually did occur. Else the entire enterprise of Judaism is based purely on a myth.

Rabbi Yisroel Chait has another slant on this concept:

> *Someone may ask how we know that these events were as described in The Torah, clearly visible, and that they transpired before the entire nation. Perhaps this itself is a fabrication? The answer to this question is obvious. We accept a simple fact attested to by numerous observers **because we consider mass conspiracy absurd**. For the very same reason no public event can be fabricated, for we would have to assume*

*a mass conspiracy of silence with regard to the occurrence of that event. If someone were to tell us that an atomic bomb was detonated over New York City fifty years ago, we would not accept it as true because we would assume that we would have certainly heard about it had it actually occurred. The very factors which compel us to accept as true an account of an event of public proportion safeguards us against fabrication of such an event. Were this not so all of history could have been fabricated. Had the event at Sinai not actually occurred, anyone fabricating it at any point in time would have met with the stiff refutation of the people, "had a mass event of that proportion ever occurred we surely would have heard of it." **Fabrication of an event of public proportion is not within the realm of credibility.***

History corroborates this point. In spite of the strong religious instinct in Man, no modern religion in over two thousand years has been able to base itself on public revelation. A modern religion demands some kind of verifiable occurrence in order to be accepted. For this reason the two major Western religions, Christianity and Islam, make recourse to the revelation at Sinai. Were it not for this need and the impossibility of manufacturing such evidence, they certainly would not have based their religions on another religion's revelation. –From Essay: *Torah From Sinai, Yeshiva B'Nei Torah*

What objections might there be to accepting this narrative reported in Torah as Truth? We cannot object by saying "nothing happened"; all of the foregoing already counters that. We might want to say, "something happened, but was misinterpreted". What are the possibilities for this?

- *"Studies show that eyewitness accounts can be inaccurate."*

For small groups of eyewitnesses, yes; for large

groups, no -- the larger the group gets, the easier it gets to sort out accurate observations (since these will be the ones that are widely repeated) and the easier it gets to identify and discard inaccurate ones (those which only few individuals assert); for 1.2 million eyewitnesses present at Sinai, the necessary crosschecking is assured.

- *"The witnesses were in a highly excited state and are thus unreliable."*

The large number of witnesses tends to offset this effect, however, the related miracle which best lends itself to this analysis is the Manna from heaven. The first time it appeared, yes, everyone was excited; the next several times they started getting used to it. Torah records that the Manna kept coming for 40 years. By then, it's pretty safe to assume that the people had pretty well gotten over the initial novelty of the thing and would have been rather accustomed to dealing with its nature. Similarly with the observation that after 40 years, nobody's garments wore out.

In addition, virtually the entire Book of Deuteronomy provides a transcript of an address Moses gave to the entire congregation of Israel after the 40 years of wandering in the Wilderness, and just prior to the final entry into the Land of Israel. This discourse provides verification of all of the prior events, including the Revelation at Sinai, leading up to that point, and was disputed by no one either at that point or later.

- *"Natural events happened but were misinterpreted at the time."*

What does the Bible say happened?

The Source of Moral Authority

EXO. 19: 16 And it came to pass on the third day in the morning, that there were thunders and lightnings, and a thick cloud upon the mount, and the voice of the trumpet exceeding loud; so that all the people that were in the camp trembled. ... 18 And mount Sinai was altogether on a smoke, because the Lord descended upon it in fire: and the smoke thereof ascended as the smoke of a furnace, and the whole mount quaked greatly. 19 And when the voice of the trumpet sounded long, and waxed louder and louder, Moses spake, and God answered him by a voice. EXO. 20: 1 And God spake all these words, saying, [2-17 The Ten Commandments] 18 And all the people saw the thunderings, and the lightnings, and the noise of the trumpet, and the mountain smoking:

What natural phenomena could account for this?

"Thunderings and lightnings" Easy - a thunderstorm.

"Whole mount quaked greatly" That's obviously an earthquake.

"Fire and ascending smoke (v.18)" That's obviously a volcano.

"Trumpet ... louder and louder (v.19)" A geyser near the volcano could sound like that.

"God spake [10 Commandments]" Hmmm. Maybe it was really Moses.

Let's take a closer look. Thunderstorm? Perhaps, but they'd seen thunderstorms before; why make a big deal over this one? Earthquake? Maybe, except that that part of the world is fairly inactive, seismically, which also causes problems in trying to explain the parting of the Red Sea and the collapse of the walls of Jericho as the results of earthquakes. Volcano? Slight problem here – Once a volcano forms, it becomes a permanent geological feature and we should be able to easily locate it today, but **THERE ARE NO VOLCANOS IN THE SINAI DESERT** or anywhere else nearby, and no evidence that there ever were any. Ditto for geysers. Moses talking instead of God? To all 1.2 million people, over the sound of thunder, "trumpet", "volcano", and Earthquake? Not likely. Also unlikely is that a thunderstorm, earthquake, volcano and geyser would all naturally occur at exactly the same time and place.

- *"Counterexample: some people falsely assert that the Holocaust never happened and are believed by many."*

This is a case of someone falsely asserting that an unusual publicly witnessed event *didn't* happen. Our case involves someone allegedly falsely asserting that an unusual publicly witnessed event *did* happen. Also, their false assertion about the Holocaust is not believed by any entire nation. The two cases are different, and the counterexample does not apply.

- *"Counterexample: people believed in dragons and goblins for a long time."*

This involves the belief of accounts of unusual events (creatures) that were purportedly seen by an individual or small groups of people, *not* large public gatherings, and certainly not whole societies. This kind of false belief is specifically the kind that *will* be believed if the storyteller is sufficiently skillful. Also, this sort of "private revelation" is the type of story upon which all religions *other than* Judaism are based.

- *"Jesus was supposed to have performed miracles before large crowds, in a situation similar to the revelation at Sinai, so why does Judaism then reject Christianity?"*

The Source of Moral Authority

It's not particularly on scrutiny of the reports of these purported miracles that Judaism rejects Christianity, but rather on various theological doctrines espoused in the New Testament, on the failure of Jesus to fulfill several basic prophecies regarding the Messiah, and also on the basis of the reports of the trial of Jesus, that, according to the way it was reported in the gospels, was done in violation of many precepts of Jewish Law, which violations would never have been tolerated in a real Jewish court.

- *"If there were so many witnesses, why is there only one account passed down?"*

Actually, there *were* several accounts. They were collected together and included in the *Midrash*, which became part of the Talmud. The Talmud is a general compendium of the *Mishna* (statements derived from the Oral Law, given to Moses at Mt. Sinai along with the Written Law (Written Torah)), the *Gemara* (analysis of the Mishna and minutes of legal arguments before the *Sanhedrin*, the "Supreme Court" of ancient Israel), the Midrash (anecdotal accounts, and homiletic and allegorical illustrations of Torah principals and assertions), and explanatory commentaries on all the above.

- *"If the story was made up long after the events supposedly happened, then lack of public common knowledge about them wouldn't discourage people from believing."*

Imagine that I'm the most credible and believable authority for information that you have at your disposal, say, the Encyclopedia Britannica. Now, suppose I tell you in this year's edition (I never said this before), "*at the time the Magna Carta was signed in 1215 at Runnymede,*

England, the sun shone blue over all England, and everyone witnessed it and everyone was astounded by it." Suppose that NO other information source at your disposal also says this. Do you believe it? After all, this is the EB, shouldn't you believe what it says? I suggest that even if it is the EB, you wouldn't and shouldn't believe it, not if *nobody* else at all can independently confirm it, especially if the event in question was alleged to have been witnessed by the entire population of the society, and no contemporaneous evidence exists to confirm it. And if someone with less credibility than EB made these assertions, then you *certainly* wouldn't believe them.

Conversely, the Torah tradition was transmitted among various Jewish communities around the world who were not in contact with each other for long periods of time. Later, when they did come in contact, it was found that their various traditions all agreed with each other on all significant matters. This, again, confirmed the veracity of the various traditions.

Within Orthodox Judaism, the Oral Torah or Oral Law is recognized as having been originated through direct connection with God. The core of the Oral Torah is clarifying information given by God to Moses while he was up on Mt. Sinai. Additional information consists of explanations of the laws as given by revered Elders.

The Oral Law, transmitted from Moses to Joshua and the Elders of Israel, was widely distributed throughout the population. I.e., a large number of individuals, in the thousands, memorized the entire Oral and Written Laws, including all the contents of the Talmud as it existed at the time (basically everything except the minutes of the later Sanhedrin cases and the commentaries). It's simply not possible that someone could come along many years after the fact and make up a story about events at Sinai that would conflict with all the memorized accounts, and then have it accepted. Especially not if all the memorized accounts are collaborative with each other.

What about the idea that all these accounts are memorized? Can't memories be faulty? Don't we all know about the "telephone game"? There are two factors to consider here:

1. There were many separate, independent, parallel channels of transmission of the Oral Law, yet all were found to be in agreement with each other when they were later gathered together, after the start of Diaspora. This was an indication that the various separate channels of memory remained true to the original information.

2. The people entrusted with transmitting the Oral Law did have demonstrably superior memories. For example, there was a game widely played by the yeshiva students of Europe up through the 19th century, and some people are still capable of playing it today. They would randomly select a volume of the Talmud. (Have you ever seen the Talmud? It consists of about two dozen volumes, each the size of a library atlas, printed in a reasonably small type font with two different Hebrew scripts.) They would open the volume to a page at random, select a word on the page at random, and then stick a pin through the page at the selected word, and into several pages behind the one at which the book was opened. The object of the game was to predict which word on each page through which the pin had passed would have a pinhole in it, on both sides of each of the pages. On top of this, none of the yeshiva students of those times used the languages written in the Talmud, Hebrew and Aramaic, as his native language. Pretty good memories, I'd say.

Other traditionally mentioned indications of the Truth of Torah and other Jewish beliefs follow, but they would be regarded as weaker evidence than the foregoing.

- There are numerous instances in Torah where faults of its patriarchal protagonists or military defeats of the Children of Israel are chronicled. Historically, this is very much out of place as compared to contemporaneous literature. Other writings of that era invariably portray the heroes as faultless, and the nations whose epics were being told as always victorious.

- The Dietary Laws (LEV. 11, DEUT. 14) indicate classes of creatures which may be eaten in terms of some general characteristics. E.g., land animals must have cloven (split) hooves and they must "chew their cud" (regurgitate partially digested food to be further chewed and swallowed); fish must have both fins and scales. Certain exceptional animals are specifically enumerated as having some of the signs of being acceptable but not others. E.g., the pig has the cloven hoof but does not chew its cud; the rabbit and the camel each chew their cud, but do not have the cloven hoof.

  One would reasonably expect that in the thousands of years since Torah was written, given all the new lands and seas discovered since then, and the thousands of new species of creatures discovered in these lands and seas, that other exceptional creatures would have been discovered. We would reasonably expect that at least some new creatures would have been found by now that also only partially fit the categories specified in Torah, like pigs and rabbits, and there might be some question if they were kosher (acceptable). But the fact is, none ever has.

Also, the Dietary Laws specify that acceptable fish must have both fins and scales. In the Talmud a rabbi is reported as saying that based on inferences derived from Torah, no fish would ever be found that has scales, but no fins. And no such fish has ever been found. Is it reasonable to expect that if men wrote Torah thousands of years ago, that they were such good psychics that they could have predicted the characteristics to be found in all newly discovered animals over the next several millennia?

- Traditional narratives of a Great Flood with similarities to that described in Torah, in various forms, occur in many other societies.

- There is great consistency with archeological discoveries. To date, no archeological discoveries have been discovered that contradict Torah.

- Torah contains information which must have been incomprehensible to people to whom it was originally given, but is eminently understandable to a modern audience. Please see **APPENDIX-2** for an example of this.

To have a fair trial, at this point we need to also consider the evidence and some of the usual arguments against the existence of God, and/or the veracity of Torah. I used to pretty much subscribe to these arguments myself. Also, how did I come to reject them? We've implicitly mentioned some of it above, but let's look at it explicitly here:

- *"If Torah indicates that God is the source of Goodness, why is there so much evil and suffering?"*

This is a classic question. The answer has to do with

God allowing Mankind to have Free Will. He gave us His Commandments, but He does not force us to obey them; we have the Free Will to obey them or not. The general consequence of disobedience of the Commandments is the generation of Evil. To the extent that Man goes against God's Commandments, Evil will triumph. This answer rests in a logical necessity for God to allow Man to have Free Will. If God does not allow Man to have Free Will, then the existence of Man is truly pointless. People would be nothing but puppets acting out a script whose conclusion God already knows, and all history and individual achievement would just be a waste of time. If Man does have Free Will, however, it makes sense in terms of a statement in Torah, DEUT. 14:1 "*Ye are the children of the Lord your God*". Presumably children will eventually grow up to become like their parents, and if that's the case here, then Man needs to learn how to exercise Free Will to properly handle the power he is even now gathering through burgeoning technology. When Man mishandles that Free Will, then the result is Evil.

- "*Why, then, do people suffer from natural disasters? They aren't generated by Evil, are they?*"

That's a good question. From a secular perspective, it would seem that one thing can't have anything to do with the other in this regard. Torah would seem to indicate otherwise. For example, in Genesis 6, we are explicitly told that the Great Flood was caused by God because of prevalent Evil among the people in the land. So, the Torah perspective is that there is a spiritual dimension to Evil that can have an effect on the natural order.

Another part of the understanding of the existence of Evil in a world created and managed by a benevolent

God, particularly injuries produced by accident, and the apparent prosperity of evil people vs. the suffering of the good, has to do with the concept that the physical world is not the last stopping point for Man's existence, but that the soul goes beyond that. That being the case, the physical world would seem to be a training ground for the soul, and that its experiences here prepare it for something else beyond the life we know. (E.g., DANIEL 12:2 *Many of them that sleep in the dust of the earth shall awake, some to everlasting life, and some to reproaches and everlasting abhorrence).* Allegorically, military training is often punishing and even downright abusive, but those who undergo it are being prepared for the warfare or deterrence provision environment they would have to face later. This is not a simple matter, and a good deal of study is necessary to have a really adequate grasp of it.

- *"So what if the odds against the spontaneous formation of life are very long, very improbable things happen all the time."*

Yes, they do. But some things get to be *too* unlikely. How many successive winning state lottery tickets would someone have to turn in before the lottery commission would start an investigation of them? My guess would be 3. Why? Because the odds against some one person being able to do that are so remote that it must raise suspicion, even if those winnings were legitimate. I think that if someone turned in 4 or 5 winning tickets in succession, the commission would suspend the lottery based on a virtual certainty that the winner was cheating, and not winning due to random chance. I think that if he turned in about 10 winning tickets, which would match the improbability as calculated above, then there would be no doubt that it was not due to random good luck!

Actual occurrence of something with infinitesimally low probability *is* an indication that something is wrong, that something is happening that, *given the ordinary laws of nature, should not be happening.* For example, there is a small but finite probability that all the air molecules in a room will spontaneously suddenly rush to one corner of the room. The probability is so small that as a matter of practical reality, it cannot happen. If it did happen, then that would be evidence that something is wrong, something other than the normal laws of nature were in play. If gross improbability weren't a valid indicator that something is wrong and occurring in the face of practical impossibility, and thus needs further investigation, then the NSA, the FBI, all police agencies, not to mention lottery commissions, would be unable to assess the value of any of their observations.

The statistical tests in themselves do not establish what higher probability entities might be responsible for the facts as found. But they do indicate the appropriateness of looking for further evidence. Let's turn it around, though. Suppose that someone came up with a mathematical analysis that indicated that the odds are 10^{75} *against* the existence of God. Honestly now, how likely would it be for an atheist to dismiss that analysis the same way that he might want to dismiss it with regard to spontaneous development of cellular life?

- *"The Bible contains descriptions of events which are clearly logically or physically impossible, such as Noah gathering samples of all the land animals of the Earth onto the ark. These are always justified as 'miracles' by Bible-believers, but there's no basis to believe they are true, and their inclusion in the Bible destroys its credibility."*

Granted, there are occurrences described in the Bible which go against our understanding of nature and physics, such as Noah's Ark and the plagues connected with the Exodus from Egypt. However, if Isaac Newton had gotten a hold of a 20th century physics text, he probably would have thought the Theory of Relativity was a bunch of illogical nonsense (e.g., the observed mass of an object increases as its speed approaches the speed of light), and had he been able to observe relativistic effects for himself, he might have thought them to be miracles. One man's miracle is just another's technology. *"Any sufficiently advanced technology is indistinguishable from magic."* – Arthur C. Clarke

- *"The Bible contains many contradictory or otherwise erroneous passages, which also destroy its credibility"*

You have to be careful in looking at "contradictions" and other "errors" in Torah. For example: DEUT. 25:19 *"... thou shalt blot out the remembrance of Amalek from under heaven; thou shalt not forget [it]."* How can we "blot out the remembrance of Amalek from under heaven", but then "not forget [it]"? We've got to assume that Whoever wrote that *must* have been aware of the apparently contradictory nature of that statement! In this case, "remembrance of Amalek" means reference to the line of people who preserve the familial "remembrance" of the ways of Amalek. "Not forget" refers to Commandments (specified elsewhere) to destroy that nation if and when the opportunity comes up.

In general, the "verses" you see in Torah need to be thought of somewhat like a series of newspaper headlines. The actual articles behind these "headlines" are compiled in the Oral Law (which has been partially reduced to writing in the form of the Talmud.) That being the case, it becomes easy to understand why there might be apparent "contradictions" and other seeming "errors" in Torah. For example, in a modern newspaper, it's common to find examples such as where one headline says, "*Experts say economy is weak*", whereas elsewhere another headline might say "*Experts say economy is strong*". Once you read the articles, you would normally see that one set of experts is talking about short term prospects, whereas the other set of experts is talking about long term prospects, and there is no real contradiction.

- *"Science tells us that the Big Bang occurred about 14 billion years ago, but Torah indicates that Creation occurred only a bit under 5800 years ago. Science has a great deal of evidence in its favor."*

The answer to this centers on an understanding of the 6 "days" (Heb. *yomim*) of Creation, what they actually were, and what actually took place during those events. As with English, the word "day" can be used in a generic symbolic sense, for example, to indicate "epoch" or "era", as in "the Day of the Dinosaur". The bottom line is that these "days" must be understood as events that are not days as we experience them, but rather they are time or time-like periods in a different dimension from our own time, but relevant to God's "environment". E.g., since the sun was not created until the Fourth "Day", then obviously the first three "days", at least, cannot have been days as we understand the term. These *yomim* are probably as different from our days as our time dimension is from our space dimensions. Also, given that the purpose of Torah is to introduce Mankind to Moral Law, then, to my mind, at least, it would seem that what was actually created during these *yomim* were the Laws governing the items being discussed, rather than those things themselves, consistent with the rendering of Moral Laws later in the text. I believe the narrative was expressed the way it is so that Torah could be understandable to ancient people who did not have knowledge of concepts like Laws of Physics. The essential idea is that the events contained within the reported *yomim* all occurred 5800 years ago from our view of time, and one of those "events" was the creation of 14 billion years of physical history along with the Creation of Man. (Please look at **APPENDIX-1** for details on this.)

- *"Modern analysis ('Higher Biblical Criticism') indicates that the Torah text was developed by being edited by people from earlier 'J', 'E', 'P' and 'D' documents."*

This is a very involved theory that suffers from a major deficiency: none of these postulated earlier documents has ever been found, and there is no evidence at all that they ever really existed. It's nothing more than an elaborate effort to theorize that Torah must have been authored by multiple people rather than by God Himself.

- *"Some laws in Torah are inherently unreasonable or unworkable, e.g., EXO. 21:23 But if any harm follows, then thou shalt give life for life, eye for eye, tooth for tooth, hand for hand, foot for foot, ..."*

This criticism comes from a lack of understanding of the context of the statements. For example, obviously, if someone is blinded, it does him no good for a court's judgment to be to likewise blind the person who might have caused his blindness. Rather, a monetary value for the loss of sight must be assessed by the court, and that amount must be charged against the perpetrator of the blindness and given to the victim.

- *"If God created the universe, then what created God? And if you say that God always existed, then why not just as well think that the universe could also have always existed, notwithstanding the argument that 'time started with the Big Bang'?"*

The flaw I find in thinking behind this argument is the assumption that God's existence is the same kind of existence as that of the material universe which we observe. There is evidence to believe that this assumption is a poor one. The evidence is that consistently, in Biblically and otherwise historically reported interactions between people and God, people have observed that God apparently has the ability to act outside the normal laws of nature, and that would be an indication that God's existence is somehow different from that of the physical universe, or "nature".

One way that God's existence could be understood to be different from that of the material universe is if one considers that God might not be constrained by the four dimensional space-time continuum in which the universe resides, but is rather an Entity that dwells in a fifth (or higher) dimensional realm. This is a very difficult concept to visualize. A nice allegory that helps explain what happens when a higher dimensional entity interacts with a lower dimensional universe is *Flatland*, by Edwin Abbott, written in 1884. If God is a higher dimensional Entity, that can explain how God is not constrained by time, nor the time-related concept of causality, as we are. That being the case, we can understand how it is that God "has always existed" whereas the physical universe has not.

- *"The perceived design in the universe exists only in the mind of the perceiver."*

The Source of Moral Authority

Those who cite this argument like to point out that there are noticeable "imperfections" in the design and conclude that the design is there essentially only because we want it to be there to provide evidence of a Designer. This is the Ultimate Denial argument. The denial lies in the cognitive dissonance in the minds of those who postulate that all that exists in the universe does so as a result of random interactions within the constraints of the laws of nature among its physical constituents. They are then faced with rigorous statistical analyses of these interactions which indicate that random interactions cannot have caused the results that we observe. This fact of gross improbability of the outcomes observed among the products of the supposed random interactions is the design we perceive.

It comes as a consequence of the very science that the deniers seek to use to deny the existence of the design. This science is very much *external* to the minds of the perceivers. So, on the one hand, the deniers postulate that the universe in general, and life in particular, are the results of random interactions of the elemental entities within the universe. But on the other hand, mathematics and science indicate that given the known laws of physics and chemistry, it is not reasonable to conclude that random interactions would produce the observed universe and life. This is the conflict leading to the cognitive dissonance, and thence to the denial.

- *"The concept that Man has Free Will, but that God has knowledge and control of future events is self-contradictory and illogical."*

Without an understanding that God exists and operates in a higher dimensional "space" than does Man, that would be a valid observation. However, if we realize that from His viewpoint, originating outside of our space-time continuum, He can view Man's past, present, and future all simultaneously, and He can likewise control them all simultaneously, then the idea that God can see and control events across time comes into focus.

So, how does Free Will fit in here? The idea is that at any moment of Man's "present", he has Free Will to do whatever he wants, but God is aware of what that choice is, and He has control of whatever the *outcome* will be for that choice. E.g., you are free to aim a gun at a target, and pull the trigger, but God then controls if the gun will fire, and if it does, what will be the result of the travel of the bullet. The really tough thing to comprehend about this is the fact that this happens for all occurrences of the "present", throughout all time. This, unfortunately, is rather alien to our experience, making it difficult to understand or accept.

Another way to see this is to consider giving a child a choice between eating candy or a bland vegetable. Does the child have Free Will to make the choice? Yes. Do you know what choice the child will make? Realistically, yes. This provides a hint at how God can allow Man to have Free Will, yet be aware of what the choices will be, and be able to "react" accordingly.

I'm sure there's no limit to the various objections that might exist to the Truth of Torah and existence of God. You will need to make your own assessment of how valid they might be, or if they're just rationalizations to justify denial of Torah.

Now, as I said, the answer to my question as to whether the evidence for the Truth of Torah was convincing is, "very likely, yes", not "certainly, yes", but the fact is, from the secular perspective, nothing is this life is absolutely certain, so I can't reasonably demand certainty in proof about the Bible and

God when I can never reasonably demand it about anything else of comparable importance in my life.

If Torah thus is accepted as Divine and Truth, then it also follows that God created the universe, since Torah says so (unless we want to assume that Torah is not telling the Truth, or that we are misinterpreting it).

Obviously, I have left out a great deal, such as how to understand the authority of the Oral Law and how the history of the Jewish people itself also provides some indication of Divine intervention. But, at least, I have covered the basics.

The rest of the logic is easy. If I am now satisfied to a reasonable probability that God exists, and that He indeed did write Torah, then I must now adapt to the facts that (a) Torah contains numerous "Commandments" (*mitzvot*) to be performed by Jews (not just the famous Ten of Exodus, but all the other "Thou shalt"s and "Thou shalt not"s enumerated around the text, some 613), and (b) by virtue of definitions derivable from Torah, I am a Jew. Also included within several of these Commandments is the requirement to transmit them to succeeding generations, e.g., *DEUT. 6:6 And these words, which I command thee this day, shall be upon thy heart; :7* ***and thou shalt teach them diligently unto thy children****, and shalt talk of them when thou sittest in thy house, and when thou walkest by the way, and when thou liest down, and when thou risest up.* The implication of these facts is that I, personally, must obey the Commandments of Torah (those that apply to me, most don't). And in order to obey these Commandments, I need to properly understand them, and this requires never-ending study, not to mention learning some of the Hebrew language, i.e., I must become an observant Jew.

How observant? Well, assuming there is some value to the continuance of Judaism and the Jewish people, which assumption comes about mostly as a consequence of acceptance of Divine Origin for Torah, then the question I asked myself was, "*If no Jew was more observant than I, then how long would Judaism and the Jewish people last?*" Sadly, the honest answer had to be, "Not long at all." Therefore, since Judaism is up to me, as much as to any other Jew, the conclusion is that I really must do my part and become more observant.

How much more observant? It's a general principle for people embarking on increasing Jewish observance that they need to "go slow". Do not try to do everything all at once; take on observances gradually. You will need to adjust your lifestyle to various new things and trying to do too many of them too soon will be overwhelming and discouraging. But the continuing spiritual reward will be great. Be aware that the observance of Sabbath (*Shabbat* or *Shabbos*) is of primary importance. In the Talmud we are told "*If a Jew observes Shabbat but no other mitzvah (Commandment), he is regarded as observant; if he observes all of the other mitzvot but not Shabbat, he is regarded as not observant*". Also bear in mind that "*No Jew comes from a long line of non-observant Jews.*" If you delve into Jewish history, you'll understand the profound significance of this.

At this juncture, I'll not go into specific procedures and mechanics of various observances. There are many other works and people who can give you authoritative guidance in that regard. I do want to make one more point relevant to the decision of whether to accept Torah as Truth, and to adopt Jewish observances.

Truth be told, I don't think that most people ever come truly to believe in God solely through rational analysis, no matter how compelling it might be. I think that something needs to happen in one's life that touches him in a special way, that makes him stop and say something like, "How can this be happening around or to *me*, if not for the Hand of God?" Then, the question of the existence of God is no longer merely an academic exercise. Then, it gets personal. That's when push comes to shove. That's when it gets to be time to jump off the fence. That's when acceptance comes. That's what happened to me. The following is part of the story of how this happened to me. Can you find anything like this in your life?

Coincidences ... Or What?

As mentioned at the beginning of this essay, I was born in the last week of the year 1944 CE in Brooklyn, New York, and lived there until my family moved to Long Island, the vast suburban area east of New York City, when I was about four years old. This is the beginning of a chain of events so astounding that had I not lived through them myself, I never would have believed this story.

When I became of age to be eligible for military service, at a point in my life when I was virtually totally devoid of religion, the Vietnam War was starting and gaining momentum. Many, if not most men of my age were in military service, or some substitute thereof. Either that, or they were busily engaged in some means of avoiding service, such as fleeing to Canada or faking some medical condition. I fit into neither of these categories. I was ready, willing, and able to join the military service of the USA. In fact, I actually attempted to join various branches of the service, yet somehow ...

All through my early life, my family was one of modest financial means, to say the least. I knew that, despite doing very well in school, if I would ever attend college, it would have to be through scholarships or some other forms of financial assistance. When I was 15 years old in 1960, during the summer between my sophomore and junior years in high school, my father was killed by a hit-and-run drunk driver (who later turned himself in). Aside from the emotional trauma engendered by this, the financial effects were equally devastating since the life insurance proceeds were indeed not overly substantial.

Whatever difficulties I was going to have in getting into college were compounded now. I did, however, think of one possible solution. The United States Air Force had recently (1955) opened its own service academy in Colorado, its own version of West Point or Annapolis. I was always fascinated by space travel, and the opportunity to participate in the US space program, through the Air Force, was a possibility I could not ignore. And to make matters even better, if I would go to the Air Force academy, not only would all my tuition, room, board, and books be paid for, courtesy of the US Taxpayer Corps, but I would be paid a stipend to boot! This seemed a natural.

Well, almost a natural. There was a little matter of my not being the most athletic kid on the block, or in town. What strengths I had in academics, (which were enough to enable me to win a New York State Regents scholarship) I more than made up for with weakness in athletics. I was always the last kid picked for any team, and first one picked-on for harassment. But I did have determination. I acquired a bar to hang across my bedroom door, and I practiced pull-ups, and push-ups, and broad jumps and all the other activities which the academy literature described in the entrance requirements. I eventually got to the point where I could do the required counts for each activity, just barely.

I applied for entrance to the Air Force Academy. If you are not familiar with that process, you need to be aware that one doesn't send an application to the institution itself, as one does with a civilian college or university. Rather, one must send the application to his local member of the US Congress, either Senate or House of Representatives. Oh yes, that's right. Appointments to US service academies are *political appointments!* It's a wonder the USA ever won a war.

While I was applying to my senators and local representatives I took heed of a lesson from the space program, which I followed as closely as I could. I observed that a spacecraft is designed to have backup systems for as many systems as possible aboard the ship, so that if a main system fails, the backup system could be employed to save the mission. More than once these backup systems did have to be used to save missions. I decided to have backups in case I was unable to make it to the Air Force Academy. I also applied to other colleges. One of them was Rensselaer Polytechnic Institute (RPI), in Troy, New York. This was, and still is, a highly rated private engineering and science school. If I were to attend there, I knew I would need to have substantial financial aid.

Part of the application process for the academy involved undergoing a "preliminary medical examination", to be conducted at a nearby Air Force base. I went for the exam, and I must say, it was one of the most thorough medical examinations I have ever had in my life. They checked everything, from head to toe. One of the tests was a blood test. I had never had a regular blood test before. On a class field trip once, I had a fingertip pin prick test for blood type. I nearly fainted, but I made it through. This time, I made the mistake of watching the blood being drawn, through a tube, into a vial. I remember thinking, "that's *me* going into that vial." When the technician finished, he told me, "OK, next stop is chest x-ray, right down the hall." I didn't feel good. I staggered down the hall. There were a few guys ahead of me in line to be x-rayed, so I decided to lean against a nearby door jamb to rest a bit. I remember the world turning into a gray mist. The next thing I knew, four gentlemen were picking me up and putting me onto a table. I had fainted. I thought, "well, it must be over for me now." But no, apparently this was not all that uncommon an occurrence. It didn't wash me out. The exam proceeded as if nothing had happened.

Finally, the word came down. I had made first alternate on my congressman's appointment list for the academy. Essentially, that meant that I was his second choice. There was still a reasonable chance that the first-choice person ahead of me might choose to go elsewhere, so it still seemed worthwhile to continue with the application process. The next stop was the "final physical and medical examination" at an Air Force base in upstate Rome, New York. Now I would finally get to show how I could do those meager pull-ups and push-ups for which I had labored so long and hard.

Three days before I was scheduled to make the journey to Rome, I got sick. It wasn't just an ordinary illness. It was measles (this was before a vaccine was available for it). I don't know if there is a good age to catch measles, but I do know that seventeen is definitely not it. I got so sick, I was afraid I was going to die. Then I got sicker and I was afraid I *wasn't* going to die. I got up once to go to the bathroom and I looked at myself in a mirror. I literally did not recognize myself, I looked so bad.

Eventually, of course, I recovered, but my trip to Rome was disrupted, and rescheduling it came to be an insurmountable obstacle. On top of that, it developed that the congressman's first choice was going to accept the appointment after all. I was not going to the US Air Force Academy for college. I was, however, accepted at RPI. Unbeknownst to me, while I was pursuing the appointment at the Air Force Academy, my brother, six years my senior, made successful efforts to secure education loans for me, for which I am extremely grateful. That, together with the Regents scholarship enabled me to go to RPI for college.

Just before I entered college, my mother decided to move back to Brooklyn. The expense of living in suburban Long Island was becoming too great for her, and now with both of her children out of the house and with her never having learned to drive, she would have been stranded in the house. She moved to Avenue X, in the southern part of Brooklyn. The significance of this will become apparent later in this story.

I entered RPI in the autumn of 1962, and signed up for a major in physics. This seemed a natural choice for me, since,

Coincidences ... Or What?

back in high school, due to various scheduling anomalies, I had taken the senior class in physics when I was in my sophomore year. I was the only 10th grader in a class of 11th and 12th graders. I came out with the top grade in the class. I took that as a signal of some sort that I was destined to be a great physicist someday. That's the way it seemed at the time, anyway.

In 1962, the storm clouds of war were gathering over Vietnam. US involvement in the conflict was slowly, but inexorably growing. Even though I was just beginning my sojourn at RPI, I felt that some planning for the future was in order. I knew it was possible that I might not be able to finish the full four years at RPI, and that even if I did, I might have to face military service upon graduation. I decided to join the Reserve Officers' Training Corps (ROTC).

ROTC (affectionately known as "rot-see") enabled a student to study Army, Navy or Air Force "military science" part time throughout the four years of school, with some full-time involvement during summers. At graduation time, the ROTC student would come out with a "reserve" commission in the branch of the service associated with his particular ROTC program, and he would enter the service as a commissioned officer, a Second Lieutenant (or Ensign in the Navy). That looked like a pretty good deal to me. If the war was still going on by the time I graduated, I would be able to go into the service as an officer, rather than a draftee enlisted person. If the war was over at that point, I might still have an opportunity to become involved with the space program if I were an Air Force officer. So, off I went to join the Air Force ROTC.

The first order of business in mustering in for Air Force ROTC was to be fitted with a uniform, which all ROTC cadets wear. Very quickly, they ran into a problem with my shoes. Now, my shoe size at that time was approximately

10½-D. That's by no stretch of the imagination an outlandish shoe size. It's a rather ordinary size. Yet, somehow, the Air Force quartermasters at RPI were unable to accommodate it. "You'll have to reapply next semester," they told me. I was not impressed. I decided to take my chances at that point, so I set aside efforts to join the military. I turned 18 at the end of that calendar year and had to sign up for "Selective Service", military conscription, the "draft". Since I was in school, I was given a student deferment (exemption).

The years went by at RPI and my dreams of becoming some great physicist were beginning to face reality. Whereas in elementary and high school, I was always able to make top grades with little effort, such was not the case at RPI. I don't know if it would have been different at another college, but I found learning very difficult at this college. The work was just plain much harder than anything I had imagined in high school. I struggled to barely maintain grades in the top quarter of the class. I even dropped a senior year solid state physics course that I was failing, and only because I had taken an extra psychology course as a freshman was I able to graduate. And then, it was only because the physics department head was doing me a favor in allowing that psych. course to substitute for the dropped physics course.

It was now 1966. The Vietnam War was coming to a boil. I was ready to enlist, if necessary, but I wanted to make one last try at being some kind of physicist, so I applied to graduate schools. Somehow, I was accepted into the physics program at Purdue University, in West Lafayette, Indiana. I had fears that graduate school would be as much more difficult than college, than college was compared to high school. It wasn't quite that bad, but still, the struggle was daunting.

At the end of the first year, I finally faced the reality that I wasn't going to earn a living as a physicist, and I switched into mechanical engineering. As "luck" would have it, the branch of mechanical engineering in which assistantship money was available to me was rocket propulsion engineering. I was studying "rocket science". As a result of that, I can now say with some authority "it's not rocket science" when the need arises. But little else. I found the study obtuse and boring. It was taught at a monstrously low level of abstraction, as compared to physics and math courses that I had had. We actually had to come out with numeric rather than algebraic answers to questions!

One good outcome of my stay at Purdue was that there I met the lady who was to become my wife. The classes were becoming more than I could bear and we decided that we would drop out at the end of my second year and get married.

Before doing that, though, I wanted to make one last attempt to join the Air Force, as an alternative to being exposed to the draft. It was now 1968 and the war in Vietnam was at full boil. I visited the US Air Force recruiter in Indianapolis to see about joining the Officer Candidate School (OCS) program. During World War II, OCS was responsible for producing the "90-Day Wonders", men who became officers after just three months of training. I believe the course was somewhat expanded since then, but it was still a very condensed version of the training one received at one of the academies. I took yet another thorough medical examination and went through a battery of written tests designed to discover what kind of aircraft pilot aptitude I might have. I called back a few weeks later to check on the progress of my application and was told that everything was going well, and that I had scored very highly on the written tests.

Shortly thereafter, my betrothed and I left Purdue, got married, and took up residence in her hometown, Randolph, Massachusetts, south of Boston. All during college and graduate school, I had had a student deferment from the draft. Now that I was out of school, my draft status became 1-A, completely eligible for the draft. I called the Air Force in Indianapolis again to check on my application to OCS. Their response was "Huh?" They didn't know who I was. They couldn't find any OCS application under my name or even similar names that are often mistaken for mine. My application paperwork was lost.

What to do now? I was not of a mind to evade the draft, but, at the same time, I didn't want to go into military service as a draftee. There was no telling what kind of assignment I might be given, and I really didn't relish the idea of digging foxholes. My wife and I decided that it would be best if I tried to enlist. After all the bad luck I had had with the Air Force, I decided it was time to give the Army a try. I visited the Army recruiter in Randolph.

I told him, "Sir, I'd like to join your Army."

He asked, "What have you been doing up until now?"

"I've been in college and graduate school. I just got married."

"What major did you have in college?"

"Physics."

He then thumbed through an index card file for a few seconds and said, "Well, we really don't have any openings for physics majors right now. How about coming back in a few weeks and try again?"

I was absolutely flabbergasted! *What was going on here?!?!* This was an Army recruiter? I was always given to believe that an Army recruiter, especially in wartime, had the job of putting a pen into the hand of anyone capable of breathing, and getting him to sign up. And he was telling me, "... no openings for physics majors ... come back in a few weeks?" I mumbled some response to him and walked out of his office, reeling. At this point, I was really beginning to get the impression that some Power was conspiring to keep me out of the military. The Academy, ROTC, OCS, and now this? It was beginning to be too much. But yet more was to come.

At this point, I had become resigned to being drafted. I was called in to take a pre-induction physical examination. I expected to be drafted at any moment.

In the meantime, however, bills had to be paid. I had to look for a job. With a draft status of 1-A, though, I knew that this was not going to be an easy task. Who would want to hire someone in imminent jeopardy of being drafted? I decided to try to find work in sales. I reasoned that if I got a job as a commissioned salesman, my employer really would not be taking on much risk in hiring me. If I sold, I would get paid, if I didn't I wouldn't. If I got drafted, the company would only lose out on some training expenses. Also, my wife had secured a steady job as a speech therapist in the school system of Brockton, a short drive from our home. This would at least provide some income even if I started off slowly in sales.

We decided that I would try one final attempt to get into the military before being drafted. On a Wednesday, I met with my wife for lunch in Brockton, and after lunch, we went looking for a Navy recruiter, to see if perhaps he might exhibit more sanity than did the Army recruiter. We found the Navy recruiting office, the typical oversized phone booth usually employed by military recruiters in those days, and more recently, used by jiffy photograph developing companies. But there was one strange thing about this Navy recruiting office. Here we were in the middle of the day, in the middle of the week, in the middle of town (and Brockton is by no means a tiny place; its population is almost 100,000), in the middle of the war. The Navy recruiting office was closed. Inside the window it was dark, so I wasn't able to tell if it was closed for just a short while or permanently. But it was closed. Just when I wanted to join up. Again, my jaw dropped. *What was going on?!*

Back to job hunting. I scoured the newspaper want-ads and registered with employment agencies that specialized in sales. After a few weeks, I was offered a job selling copy machines.

As I was about to accept the job, I got a call from one of the employment agencies. This was a branch of the largest employment agency in the country, whose signature specialty was in placing salespeople. Strangely enough, they had a company interested in hiring a physicist. I went for the job interview. It was with a small company that was manufacturing, or more accurately, was trying to manufacture industrial lasers. Back in 1968, the laser was essentially the cure for which there was virtually no known disease. Laser technology had only been first demonstrated while I was back in college. This company had apparently acquired some funding based on the fact that they were somehow involved with a very high-profile case in which a well-known baseball player had had retinal reattachment through laser surgery. They offered me a job. At this point in history, technical people just getting out of school were normally getting salaries in the range from $7500 to $8500 per year. They offered me $10,000. I took it.

But what about the draft? The company wrote a letter to my draft board requesting an occupational deferment for me. I seemed to recall hearing at that time that due to increasing manpower requirements for the war, draft boards were no longer permitted to grant occupational deferments, so I expected the request to be denied. But mine was not just any draft board.

You see, when I turned 18 and registered for the draft back in my first year in college, my mother had already moved back to Brooklyn, hence my legal residence was there. Had my father not been killed and my mother not moved back to Brooklyn, I would have been under the jurisdiction of a Long Island draft board. Long Island was overall a relatively affluent area. Very many of its draft age men were either in school or had fled to Canada. Manpower there was in short supply for filling draft board quotas. Anyone who was around that had 1-A status would immediately be drafted, no ifs, ands or buts.

But I was not under the jurisdiction of a Long Island draft board. Instead, I was now under the jurisdiction of the draft board of a different "island", Coney Island, which, no matter where I later resided, would always have jurisdiction over me. This draft board covered a large section of southern Brooklyn, including Ave. X, where my mother lived, and where my legal residence was, when I registered with them. Much of the other territory covered by this draft board is what is called these days "Inner City Depressed Urban Ghetto". A large segment of the population consisted of unemployed men who provided an ample pool of manpower for the draft. This draft board never had problems filling its quotas. They granted me the occupational deferment.

Again, it seemed, civilian-hood had been snatched from the jaws of the military. And it wasn't quite over yet. During the next eight months at the laser company, I never really did any work as a physicist, but I did start using computers. I parlayed a little computer experience I had picked up in college and graduate school and worked it into a full-scale computer programming skill.

After eight months of never succeeding in selling a laser system, the laser company went out of business. I then got a job as a computer programmer for a soils engineering software company, at a salary $2000 higher than what I was making at the laser company. They also requested an occupational deferment for me, and it was granted. Six months later, that company also went out of business, and I was then able to get a job with the computer service vendor that the software company was using. They paid me $2400 more than the software company was paying me, and again, they requested and received yet another occupational deferment for me.

Finally, after a couple more years, I received a notice from the Coney Island draft board ordering me to appear to discuss my draft status. By now, I was 25 years old, I had a child, and I was near the maximum age at which one could be drafted. I went down to Coney Island to the draft board office, which was as dismal and depressing as most of the area it covered. I met with a rather hostile fellow, whose poor disposition might have been due to his inability to secure a decent toupee to cover his shiny head. He reviewed my draft board records and made a comment, "It looks to me like you've been trying, in the worst way, to beat the draft with all of these student and occupational deferments!"

"Hold on!" I told him. "Exactly the opposite is true", and I went on to give him the whole litany of my attempts to enter the service, from the Air Force Academy, to ROTC, to OCS, to the Army recruiter, to the Navy recruiting office. I was almost yelling at him. "Trying to evade? I've been trying every which way to get in! I didn't run to Canada! I'm here! Take me!"

"Oh, we're gonna get ya, all right!" he snarled. "Fine!" I said, "You have my address and phone number. I'll be there. Goodbye". I expected to be drafted within the week. I never heard from them again. I have no idea why.

So, there it is. Every opportunity I had to join the military was thwarted one way or another. Are these merely coincidences? It sure seems contrived to me. Judaism says that there is no such thing as coincidence. What can I say?

But there is one more incident I would like to relate, and if there is no such thing as coincidence, then what would it be?

In 1990, around the time of Passover, I started searching for a part time position to supplement my income. As the search was going on, I began to get symptoms of a severe toothache. I went to a dentist. He found a cracked filling, which he repaired, but the pain persisted. I went back and he performed some more extensive tests. His verdict was that I didn't have a toothache after all, but rather I was developing a relatively uncommon neurological condition known as *trigeminal neuralgia*. This ailment also goes under another name, *tic doloroux* (pronounced tik da-la-ROO), which means "painful spasm" in French.

After a few weeks of searching and coming to terms with my trigeminal neuralgia, I finally was offered a part time position. It occurred on the 33rd day after the start of Passover, on a day known in Judaism as *Lag B'omer*. But that's not the coincidence that I intended to highlight. It turned out that the company that hired me at that point was a subsidiary of another company. This parent company was a British company with a French name. That name was *de la Rue*. Get it? While I was suffering from *tic doloroux*, I was hired by a subsidiary of *de la Rue*! Both names are pronounced virtually the same. What are the odds of that combination of circumstances coming together by chance? Rather long, I would imagine.

Conclusion

If, before you started reading this work, you were convinced that acceptance of the existence of God could only come through blind faith, I hope I've ruined your day. It's not that I want to cause you suffering, but I do want you to experience some discomfort with the heretofore comfortable idea you might have had that you could dismiss religious belief as simply being based on unquestioning trust and irrational thinking.

The essential point I want to drive home is that there is a natural process that you and everyone else goes through to arrive at beliefs about significant issues, aside from actual scientific experiments. This is the process of conducting trials in your mind, in which your own thinking presents both sides of an issue, and acts as judge and jury to reach a verdict. As with a real court trial, this can only work if true facts are presented, and unbiased logical evaluations of those facts are made.

I've tried to show how I applied those processes in my own life to provide an example for others. These processes are not simple, and, indeed, might require a good deal of time and effort for getting at useful conclusions. For example, it took me months to fully understand and accept that argument of how the Revelation at Sinai was similar to a major earthquake with respect to hoax immunity.

For me, at least, once I got over that hump, it was simply logical to accept that Torah, indeed, was the ultimate source of moral guidance for me, personally, and for the world in general. For you, I believe, it will be an exercise in honest self-analysis of your own thinking to see if you come to similar conclusions. I hope you will.

Appendix-1

Torah *IS* Law

It's a well-known principle of Torah study that one cannot simply read the plain text of Torah without explanation, particularly the Book of Genesis, and find it obviously understandable. The extreme example of this is where plants are created on the Third Day of Creation, but the sun, which one would expect to be necessary for the growth of the plants, is not created until the Fourth. It would seem that it should be the other way around.

It strikes me that by making a relatively small adjustment in the way the text is viewed, it can go a very long way to solving these kinds of problems. To begin with, we note that this body of knowledge is called Torah, which in Hebrew means Law or Instruction. If we bear in mind that the Torah is indeed telling us about Law(s) rather than about physical events, many otherwise seemingly disjoint items suddenly fall into logical place. For example, suppose we are from Nepal or Mars or somewhere else Torah has never before been seen, we open a Torah text and start to read:

> *GEN. 1:1-2 IN THE beginning God created the heaven and the Earth. Now the Earth was unformed and void, and darkness was upon the face of the deep; and the spirit of God hovered over the face of the waters.*

If we just read this plain text, we are perplexed: if the Earth was unformed and void, that is a description of a Nothing. Did He create Something or Nothing? If the Earth was "void", how was there water? How did hovering over the face of the waters work? And if the sun didn't exist yet, it would have been very cold, and the water would have had to be ice. Well, we are told that comets are largely ice, but they orbit around the sun, and without the sun yet existing, this is

Appendix-1

still mysterious.

But let's reread the passage with the idea in mind that we are being told about law:

> *GEN. 1:1-2 IN THE beginning God created [the law by which] the heaven and the Earth [would come into existence]. Now the [law of] Earth was unformed and void [i.e., initially without specifics], and [without further details of the law] darkness was upon the face of the deep; and the spirit of God hovered over the face of the waters.* [I think this last phrase is a hint that here is where God establishes the laws governing gravitation (embodied in "hovered over"), a very fundamental component of the universe, and also an indication of the importance of water, which will be further dealt with later.]

The idea here is that in creating the physical laws by which various things will exist, God is, by implication, creating the things. In other words, the potential for the things is created through the laws, and at the proper time, they can actually come into physical being. It's expressed this way (as if the things themselves were directly being created), however, so that the information could be understandable to ancient people initially given the Torah, who were unfamiliar with concepts like Laws of Physics.

> *GEN. 1:3-4 And God said: 'Let there be light.' And there was light. And God saw the light, that it was good; and God divided the light from the darkness.*

The plain text doesn't say why He created light, and if the world was empty, except for some water, it's hard to understand why He would go to the trouble at this point. And why would light be "good"? What would be the connection between light and morality?

But in our view: *GEN. 1:3-4 And God said: 'Let there be [the law by which] light [can exist].' And there was [the law for] light. And God saw the [law for] light, that it was good [consistent with His purposes]; and God [made law that] divided the light from the darkness.*

The existence of light is a fundamental building block of existence of the universe. The theory of Special Relativity tells us that the speed of light, i.e., speed of photon travel, is an invariant constant, the same for all observers regardless of their motion with respect to the source of the light, or each other. Speed is the ratio of distance (space) divided by time. So, by establishing the law for the existence of light, God was also necessarily setting the laws by which both space and time would exist. This ties together with the laws of gravitation, and all of these are dealt with in the theory of General Relativity. Moreover, this interpretation is consistent with the fact that no source for any physical light has yet been specified.

GEN. 1:5 And God called the light Day, and the darkness He called Night. And there was evening and there was morning, one day.

This seems completely arbitrary, and again is problematic since the sun doesn't yet seem to exist.

But in our view: *GEN. 1:5 And God [created law governing time periods, in which are] called the light Day, and the darkness He called Night. And there was [the law of the] evening and [the law of the] morning, [defining] one day.*

Here, it seems, God is planning ahead for the existence of living things, whose operation, as it were, will include circadian rhythms, which will allow them to use time as a control mechanism for physiological processes of their lives.

Appendix-1

> *GEN. 1:6-10 And God said: 'Let there be [the law of] a firmament in the midst of the waters, and [to] let it divide the waters from the waters.' ... and the gathering together of the waters called He Seas; and God saw that it was good.*

In our view, God is here establishing in some detail the laws by which air and water will exist and operate in the world. Why should He be so concerned with water at this point?

Water is very special stuff. It has the very unusual property that when it cools from liquid to solid (ice) its density decreases, and the solid floats on top of the liquid. Other materials that have this property are relatively rare in the universe, such as bismuth, antimony, gallium, and plutonium. But water is composed of hydrogen and oxygen, among the most common elements in the universe. This property of water is instrumental in the support of life: among other things, it allows life in the sea to survive when the temperature becomes so cold that water freezes. The ice floats and the water below retains enough heat to remain liquid and allow life to continue.

Once the laws for the existence of water are established, the laws of plants can then be developed.

> *GEN. 1:11-12 And God said: 'Let [the law exist to allow] the Earth [to] put forth grass, herb yielding seed, and fruit-tree bearing fruit after its kind, wherein is the seed thereof, upon the Earth.' And it was so. And the [the law was established so that the] Earth brought forth grass, herb yielding seed after its kind, and tree bearing fruit, wherein is the seed thereof, after its kind; and God saw that it was good.*

Since water is critically important for the life of plants, it is eminently logical that the laws governing plants are now developed after the laws for water, so that the plants will "know" how to use the water. We see that there is a particular emphasis on the laws of genetics (generating fruit and seed "*after its kind*"), which are instrumental in allowing the life of the plants to continue over time.

Plants are truly amazing in that they combine such things as water, air, chlorophyll, soil and sunlight to produce food that other life can consume for sustenance. So, now that the laws for the existence of plants are established, including the necessary specifications for the sunlight, this is the next logical place for the laws governing the sun to be developed, so that the sun will produce the correct kind of light once it is physically created, to support plant life.

> *GEN. 1:14-19 And God said: 'Let there be [laws for] lights in the firmament of the heaven to divide the day from the night; ... And God made the [laws of] two great lights: the greater light to rule the day, and the lesser light to rule the night; and the stars.*

The physical laws governing the existence of the sun are far too complex to enumerate here, but suffice it to note that the sun produces its energy through the process of thermonuclear fusion, the same process that makes the hydrogen bomb work. In fact, the sun is essentially composed of the equivalent of billions of hydrogen bombs continuously reacting, for billions of years. (It's truly miraculous that such an object could continue to exist for longer than a microsecond, let alone billions of years!) Yet, the sun is located just far enough from the Earth so that only just enough energy reaches the Earth to support life, not more, not less. (Scientists call this "The Goldilocks Zone".) And the spectrum of that energy filtering through the Earth's atmosphere centers on visible light, having just the right spectral characteristics to allow plants to function. So, logically, it makes sense that the laws governing the sun would now be developed in view of (i.e., following) the laws necessary for the plants.

Appendix-1

But, how about the moon and the stars: how do they fit in here? For the moon, we were told in GEN. 1:14 "*and let them be for signs, and for seasons, and for days and years*". The moon is a spherical object which just happens to appear to be the same size as the sun. Yet, based purely on physical principles, there is no reason that this should be the case. After all, the moon is actually much smaller than the Earth, and the sun is far, far bigger. Yet the distance from the Earth to the moon is just right to make the moon appear from the Earth to be the same size as the sun. And the orbit of the moon revolving around the Earth causes it to show phases as time goes on. This, I believe, is part of God's plan for having the moon influence the calendar that Man will use for guidance (*for signs, and for seasons*) on conducting many observances.

And the stars? Modern science tells us that these are objects rather like our sun, some larger, some smaller, that are all also giant hydrogen-to-helium fusion furnaces. But they are so far away that their light takes many years to reach us, even though light travels at about 186,000 miles per *second*. Consequently, they all appear as tiny points of light. They are so far away that their gravitational attractions are so attenuated due to their distances from Earth that any such effects are truly infinitesimal and inconsequential. So, why would God bother with generating laws to govern their existence?

It turns out that stars have life cycles: they are born through processes we don't fully understand having to do with gravitation affecting clouds of hydrogen and some influence of the Big Bang; they form furnaces where hydrogen atoms undergo fusion to form helium atoms, emitting great quantities of heat and light energy; eventually, they burn out, then collapse, then explode (novas and supernovas). During the collapse, gravity and pressure become so great that the helium atoms crunch together and fuse to form heavier elements, all

Appendix-1

of the members of the Periodic Table of Chemical Elements. This secondary fusion process generates enough energy to cause many of the collapsed stars to explode. The resultant heavier elements are thus scattered across the universe.

But there have been so many such collapsed star explosions that large amounts of these heavier elements were able to gather together due to their own gravitational attractions, to form objects like planets, moons, asteroids and comets. Now we can see how all the Laws that God developed come full circle, i.e., the Laws of Creation and life cycles of stars combine to support the processes of the *physical* creation of the Earth and other planets, etc.

Next, (GEN. 1:20-25) God ordains the laws governing animal life, in the sea, in the air, and on land. Again, He specifies that the laws of genetics will apply to animal life, just as they would to plants. And again, we realize that these laws governing animal life logically should come after the laws which defined how plant life should exist, and how sunlight should support that plant life, since all animal life would be completely dependent, either directly or indirectly, on plant life.

Finally, for the laws of Creation (GEN. 1:26-31), comes the Creation of Man. At this point, we need to note a Midrashic statement. (The Midrash contains homiletic narratives in the Talmud.)

From Rabbi Shlomo Yitzhaki ("RASHI", a pre-eminent commentator and explainer of the Torah and Talmud), "*The world was created for the sake of Man.*" This, I believe, implies when actual physical creation occurred. I.e., physical creation occurred when God said, "*Let Us make Man...*" (GEN. 1:26), since, based on Rashi's statement, it was logically needless for the universe to exist physically without, or substantially prior to, the Creation of Man. Based on calculations of time durations of lives and events cited in Torah, the Creation

Appendix-1

of Man and the consequent creation of all physical history occurred almost 5800 years ago for *our* perspective, forming the basis for the modern Hebrew calendar.

This takes us into some rather difficult conceptual areas. In particular, how do we square the whole process of physical creation, which appears to have begun some 14 billion years ago according to scientific observation, with the six days of Creation cited in Torah, and the concept that Man was created at the beginning of the current Hebrew calendar, only almost 5800 years ago?

We can start with the well-known concept that God exists outside, or above, what we perceive of as time. I.e., all time, our past, present, and future are always accessible to Him simultaneously. To proceed further in this discussion, we need to find some way to visualize this ... no simple matter!

Imagine the top of a long dining room table. Imagine that one end of the table represents the Beginning of Time (BoT), and the other end represents the End of Time (EoT). All of history, past, present and future, lies between these two ends.

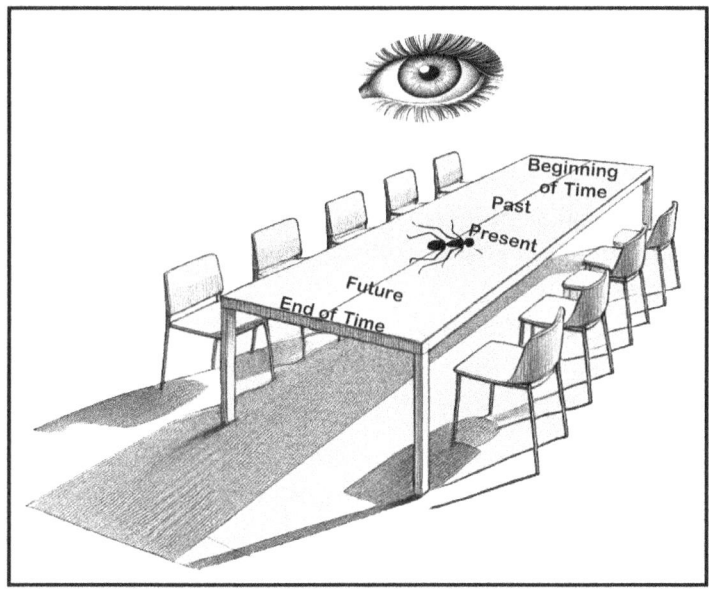

Appendix-1

Now, imagine an ant standing somewhere near the middle of the tabletop. He can only see things in the plane of the tabletop, nothing above or below.

If he looks toward the BoT end of the tabletop through his memory, he sees his past. If he looks toward the EoT end, he cannot see the future, but he can imagine that the future will largely resemble the past and the present. After all, that exercise has always pretty much worked before.

If he looks toward the sides, he sees the present world around him. In real life, he would see his present world in three dimensions (left-right, up-down, forward-back), but in our illustration here, the three dimensions are collapsed into one, so the ant would see just one spatial dimension.

The point behind setting up this ant-on-the-tabletop scenario is to allow us to imagine how God sees our world. To Him, standing above the tabletop, the ant's past, present, and future are all visible and accessible simultaneously. I.e., not only does He see the ant in the ant's present state, but He sees all of the ant's past and future states, again, simultaneously. And if He chooses, He can make changes to any and all of those past/present/future states.

The idea here is, we may visualize God as existing in a space and time outside of our own space/time world. In mathematical conceptions, we could think of God as dwelling in space/time dimensions outside (or "above") our own four-dimensional space/time continuum (three dimensions of space plus one dimension of time). These higher dimensions of space and time may well correspond to the higher Spherot ("spheres, regions") discussed in Kabbalah ("Receiving", i.e., esoteric spiritual or mystical learning).

It also can explain how it's possible that "man is created in God's image", yet individual humans can look very different from each other. The idea here is that Man is a four dimensional

Appendix-1

(three spatial and one temporal) projection of the yet higher dimensional God. Projections of higher dimensional objects onto lower dimensional spaces can easily have very diverse appearances. E.g., full face and profile photographs (two dimensional) of a person (three dimensional) look very different from each other. (A space alien who never before saw a human might not be able to guess that those two photos are of the same being.) Hence, the image (projection) of God onto our space-time continuum can easily appear as man or woman, of any race, in all kinds of mutually diverse renderings.

So, back to the question of 6 days vs. 14 billion years vs. 5800 years. If, indeed, "The world was created for the sake of Man", then again logically, there would be no requirement to have the physical world exist substantially before Man would exist. So, when God ordained that Man should come into existence, *that's* the point at which the 14 billion years of previous time and space also came into actual existence. This comports with the classic idea that God created an "old Earth" when He created Man and that He created the First Man (Adam) as an adult, not a baby, but actually, the two views are just two sides of the same coin. I.e., in creating an "old Earth", He actually also created "old everything else", i.e., all of the 14 billion years of prior physical and temporal existence.

This understanding also fits nicely with another Midrashic statement. "*God looked into the Torah and created the world.*" In the ordinary understanding of Torah as having described physical creation, this is difficult to comprehend. I.e., it says that God looked into the Torah seemingly before creating the world, but it has already been created according to that Torah. But in our understanding, that Torah contains the laws of Creation, rather than descriptions of physical creations, the statement makes perfect and obvious sense. I.e., God consulted, so to speak, His laws and recipes for proceeding with Creation by "looking into Torah", and went through the process of actually building the Laws of Creation accordingly over six "days", culminating with the physical Creation of the universe and Man on the sixth "day".

But, what about these six "days" of Creation? We can understand this if we accept the concept that God operates, as it were, in a different time dimension than the one that we experience. That time dimension does not necessarily need to resemble or operate in the same way that ours does, any more than our time dimension resembles any of our space dimensions. When Torah tells us that God did His various steps of Creation over a period of six "days", this is merely an instance of "Torah speaking in the language of Man". Actually, I believe, they are simply a linguistic mechanism for exhibiting the logical order in which the Laws of Creation were established to facilitate our understanding of the "engineering" behind them; they really have nothing necessarily to do with any actual time durations needed to create them. But, as mentioned above, they serve as a conceptual model of our own days and nights, providing the basis for the rotation of the Earth, and being comprehensible to ancient societies not yet familiar with concepts like Laws of Physics. Indeed, since the sun wasn't created until the fourth "day" of Creation, it's clear that the first three "days" could not have been days like we experience them, and presumably, likewise with the others.

Thus, on the sixth "day" of Creation, Man, along with the entire physical world around him, including all space, and all past history (from the viewpoint of the created Man) and future time, are created. I.e., this happens on the sixth "day" of Creation in God's time dimension; but all of our space and time dimensions are created at that point. And from the point of view of us people living today *within* that created history, this all occurred approximately 5800 years ago.

Appendix-1

Now, through our scientific observations, we can only see the effects of the physical creation, which appears to have begun about 14 billion years ago, with the Big Bang. We scratch our heads trying to figure out just how, physically, the Big Bang could have happened, since it appears that all of physical creation emanated instantly from a single infinitesimal point.

But, with the understanding that God can operate in other space and time dimensions beyond what we experience, we can propose a model of how the Big Bang worked. Let's return to that tabletop with the ant in the middle.

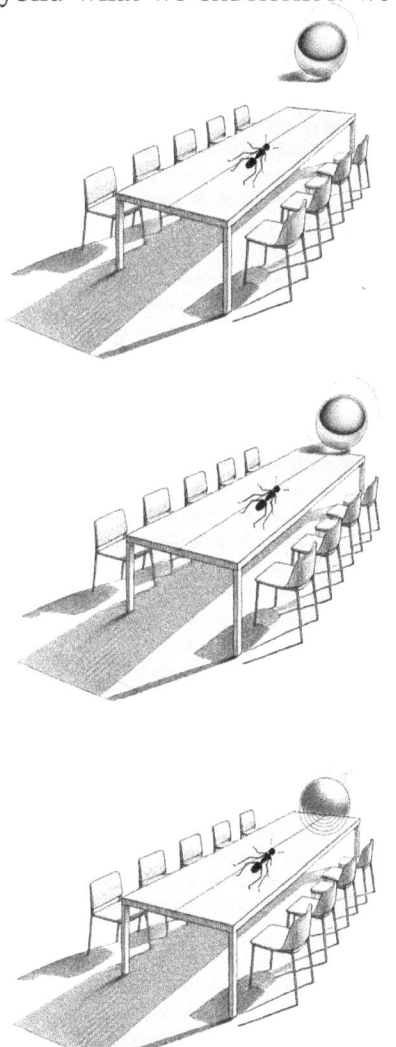

Imagine that right at the Beginning of Time end of the table there is a sphere floating above the table. Now imagine that the sphere floats down toward the table until it just touches it. Right then, the ant looking through his telescope toward that event would see a mere point, where the sphere just touches the tabletop. Now, imagine that the sphere continues descending and piercing the tabletop; the ant would see the point expanding. Now, imagine that that piercing process happens within a small fraction of a second; the ant would see that quick expansion as a Big Bang. Interestingly enough, some theoretical physicists are beginning to adopt ideas similar to this. In other words, if we just generalize the concept that God exists outside of our world of space and time, we might gain some understanding of the process of the Creation of the Laws of Existence, and the process of the physical creation of the world.

Now, we can tackle the question of just why God took the trouble to tell us these details of His process of creating the Laws governing the existence of the world. After all, He could have just as well left out all the information we discussed relating to verses GEN. 1:2 through GEN. 1:31, and continued with GEN. 2, and that would have still sufficed to provide all of the moral instruction contained in Torah.

We also note that at the completion of Creation Torah now starts using God's name of *Y-H-W-H* (rendered as *LORD* in our translation.) Traditional Torah learning explains that the name *God* refers to His attribute of judgment (or lawgiving in our context) and transcendence over the physical world, whereas *LORD* refers to His attribute of mercy and His propensity to consider mitigating circumstances. Now that Man exists with his imperfections and *yetzrim horim* (inclinations toward Evil), this additional attribute of God would be necessary to indicate in Torah in order to understand how Man could continue to survive in view of his moral weaknesses in the face of Divine judgments. And Torah would be necessary to guide Man in dealing with his defects.

We note that Torah makes a point of telling us that the seventh day (in God's time dimension) marked the completion of the Laws of the Creation process by being hallowed. For a long time I wondered why God ordained the seventh day, *Shabbat*, to be a special holy day, rather than the sixth day, which marked the final acts of Creation; after all, we normally make a *siyum* (celebration of completion of Torah segment study or other significant event) at the time when we complete a spiritually important activity. I believe that in hallowing the seventh day, when no more creations were being done, rather than the sixth day, that this was a signal to us to understand that these Laws were now complete and permanent; that they will never change within our space/time world, since likewise on this Sabbath/seventh day, nothing was created or changed. (This is in contrast to Man's laws, which are continually being amended and expanded.)

This understanding of the completeness and permanence of God's Laws (and, for that matter, of God Himself) is, I believe, central to the understanding of the importance of our observance of Shabbat. I.e., the completeness and permanence of His Laws (both physical and moral) are reflected in the completeness and permanence of Torah, and by implication, the completeness and permanence of the People who received that Torah, who will ultimately transmit its concepts to the rest of the world. ***Our observance of Shabbat is our confirmation of our understanding of that arrangement and of our part in it.***

"Completeness and permanence of the People"? What does that mean? It means the Nation of Israel does not increase its numbers by proselytizing. Also, despite being only about 0.2% of the world's population, it has a grossly outsized influence on the law, philosophy and culture of Western Civilization, on technology, and on the focus of world affairs attention, further attesting to the sufficiency of its size. It also means that despite undergoing adversities such as no other nation has survived, for over 3000 years, the Nation of Israel is still here and going strong in the face of continual challenges, attesting to its permanence.

I once attended a *shiur* in which a young rabbi from South Africa expounded a concept which I believe might be *the most difficult* concept with which to deal in Torah learning. He said that if you see something in Torah which seems wrong to you, then you must understand that Torah is not wrong, but you are, and you need to do some additional Torah learning. This is indeed a tough pill to swallow.

For example, Torah tells us not to eat the meat of pigs. As a rational person, I realize that billions of people have been eating pig meat for thousands of years, and (as long as they cook it well) there evidently have been no problems with that. OK, let's posit that for some reason eating pig meat has a negative effect on one's morality. Then we further note that the soldiers of ISIS, who are Muslims and don't eat pig meat, are still capable of the worst atrocities, so abstaining from pig meat doesn't seem to help in that regard. Therefore, on a purely rational basis, eating or abstaining from pig meat apparently has no effect one way or the other. So, why does Torah tell us not to eat it?

Ultimately, the answer is: we don't know. So, why should we heed Torah when it tells us that? This is why Torah explained the process of the Creation of the Laws of Existence. By looking at the day-by-day sequence of the Creation of the Laws, we can understand the fundamental logic of the order of the Creation of the Laws. Then, through the study of science, we can understand the phenomenal success of these Laws in governing the continuing operation of physical existence.

In other words, the operational success of the scenario of the day-by-day Creation of the Laws of Existence, as narrated in GEN. 1, together with our own scientific understanding of the success of these Laws for the workings of the universe (specifically, it would seem, for the benefit of modern scientifically informed observers), ***establishes God's credentials*** as The Transcendentally Reliable Law Maker. *When it comes to making laws, He has thus demonstrated that we can **trust** that **HE KNOWS WHAT HE IS DOING**, and His Laws are exactly correct for the moral guidance of Mankind.* So, for example, if

Appendix-1

He tells us not to eat pigs, we can trust that there is a good reason for it, even if we don't understand it.

This brings up the question of the nature of laws, and why anyone obeys any of them. For example, why stop at a red light? There are three basic reasons:

1. Fear of getting caught and punished: The person who obeys a law for this reason is just a game-player. He has no respect for the law and if he was convinced that he wouldn't get caught, then he would run the red light.

2. Agreement with the benefit of the law: This person obeys this law because he understands how it prevents accidents and death. But if he didn't agree that the law would serve some benefit, then he might not obey it and would probably go back to case (1). For this person, the law is only a recommendation, hence he is not really a law-abiding citizen either.

3. Because the law is the law: This person respects the law as such and would obey it even if he were sure he wouldn't get caught, and even if he didn't agree with the rationale for it. He might break it only in very extreme circumstances when severe mitigating factors were present. The third person is the law abiding, moral person, but even here, there might be a concern about the competence of the lawmakers to make good laws. If moral laws are made by Man then one can always believe his thinking is superior to that of the lawgivers, and therefore he can just as well make up his own morality. If, on the other hand, moral laws come from God, then one can trust that God's competence at moral lawmaking would always be better than his own, that God knows what He's doing, and that therefore following His moral laws *will* be worth it.

Appendix-1

This is why the "days" of the Creation narrative tells us about the Creation of Laws, rather than the Creation of things, and why this was disclosed to us. So, as so often happens with Torah Learning, we come full circle: Torah tells us how God created the Laws governing the existence of the world; science exposes the details of how these Laws operate; human intellect seeks to know why these Laws exist as they do; Torah tells us the logic behind the creation of these Laws. And in doing so, explains how God is the Ultimate Expert at creation of Laws. And thus, we can understand on an intellectual level, particularly even with our skeptical, secular background, the value of cleaving to His Laws; they come from a trustworthy Source and are all for our benefit.

Appendix-2

End of Heaven?

A strange choice of words occurs in the Book of Deuteronomy:

Moshe Rabbenu ("Moses, Our Teacher"), as part of his long discourse related in this Book of Torah, just prior to the people's entry into the Land of Israel, reminds them of the uniqueness of God's appearance before them at Mt. Sinai, along with the miracles of the Exodus. He poses a rhetorical question:

> DEUT. 4:32 *"For ask now of the days past, which were before thee, since the day that God created Man upon the Earth, and from the one end of heaven unto the other, whether there hath been any such thing as this great thing is, or hath been heard like it?"*

He is saying that nothing like this ever happened in history, but in saying this, he includes "since the day God created Man upon the Earth, and *from the one end of heaven unto the other [end of heaven]*" (Heb.: *ulmiktzei hashamayim v'ad ktzei hashamayim*). The question is, why put it that way?

After all, we would have expected him to say, "from one end of the Earth unto the other." Then, the entire point would have been very clear. I.e., *nothing like that ever happened from the beginning of time and anywhere on Earth*. But that's not what he says. He seems instead to say, nothing like that ever happened from the beginning of time and anywhere in heaven, which is rather hard to understand. Indeed, if something like this did occur in heaven, there would have been no person there (in heaven) to witness it, and it's not clear that such a thing

Appendix-2

in heaven could be witnessed by people on Earth. Let's look closer.

If "end of heaven" is a spatial reference and the phrase means the physical extent of the space of heaven, this seems rather out of place, as it were, since Mt. Sinai, where God came down and revealed Himself, is inherently a place on Earth. There would seem to be no way that such a thing could happen in heaven, as we don't associate any mountains being located in heaven (notwithstanding that the tops of some mountains sometimes poke into the clouds). Further, the Exodus took place in Egypt, which obviously is not in heaven.

If, however, "end of heaven" is a temporal reference, then it would seem to mean from the time heaven started to exist, until the time that heaven comes to an end, in the future. This would fit better with the concept that Moshe is asking if anything else like God's Revelation at Sinai and the miracles of the Exodus ever occurred in all of history. But if that's the case, why refer to "end(s) of heaven" rather than, say, the start and end of the Earth?

If we look at Rashi (Talmudic commentator), he only says that the plain meaning of the text is to be understood as is, but that there is a Midrashic interpretation referring to the idea that Adam was tall enough to be able to reach up to heaven, and that height was the same as the breadth of heaven. This doesn't seem relevant to the question at hand.

We can look further for a possible *Gezeira Shava* ("similar decree", i.e., inference from the occurrence of the same expression elsewhere in Torah). Indeed, this expression does occur just once more in Torah:

> DEUT. 30:4 *If any of thine that are dispersed be in the uttermost parts of heaven (Heb: biktzei hashamayim), from thence will the LORD thy God gather thee, and from thence will He fetch thee.*

If anything, this would seem to make matters even more confusing. Why?

If we look at all of the references in Torah to "heaven" (*Shemayim*), we find that it's a place where God and the angels might dwell, where the sun, moon, stars and planets are found (which is why they're called "heavenly bodies"); and from whence wind, rain and snow come. But nowhere in Torah do we find any indication that people might live there ... *except right here*. It explicitly says that if any of the exiles of the Diaspora are there, at the time of Redemption, God will gather them even from there. It's the only reference in Torah like it, indicating that people might be dwelling in heaven.

(There is another reference a little further down:)

DEUT. 30:11-12 *For this Commandment which I command thee this day, it is not too hard for thee, neither is it far off. It is not in heaven, that thou shouldest say: 'Who shall go up for us to heaven, and bring it unto us, and make us to hear it, that we may do it?'*

This seems to indicate that some people might be thought of as able to visit heaven [and attend yeshiva there?], but it doesn't seem to indicate that people might live there on any ongoing basis.)

So, how can we understand this? Well, as always, we look to Rashi. What does he say about this? NOTHING! His commentary on the Torah completely skips over this verse. The same is true of Nachmanides and other commentators. What's going on here?!?!

Let's put ourselves in the place of people who lived a few hundred years ago or more. How could they have understood that passage? Certainly, they could not understand it literally, since there was no way people then could even fly, let alone travel into space or live there. Back then, they didn't even really have a concept of what outer space is.

At best, they might have understood it allegorically, with a meaning like, "*Even if the exiles have become extremely far removed from Torah teachings and practices, they will still be redeemed.*" But they could not have understood it as meaning that people could literally live in heaven.

I once asked a rabbi if various parts of the Torah were intended to be understood in different ways by different audiences, hearing it at different times. For example, for us, today, the passages about the Red Heifer are extremely difficult to understand and require complex explanations:

> *NUM. 19:1 And the LORD spoke unto Moses and unto Aaron, saying: :2 This is the statute of the law which the LORD hath commanded, saying: Speak unto the children of Israel, that they bring thee a red heifer, faultless, wherein is no blemish, and upon which never came yoke. :3 And ye shall give her unto Eleazar the priest, and she shall be brought forth without the camp, and she shall be slain before his face. :4 And Eleazar the priest shall take of her blood with his finger, and sprinkle of her blood toward the front of the tent of meeting seven times. :5 **And the heifer shall be burnt in his sight; her skin, and her flesh, and her blood, with her dung, shall be burnt. :6 And the priest shall take cedar-wood, and hyssop, and scarlet, and cast it into the midst of the burning of the heifer. :7 Then the priest shall wash his clothes, and he shall bathe his flesh in water, and afterward he may come into the camp, and the priest shall be unclean until the even. :8 And he that burneth her shall wash his clothes in water, and bathe his flesh in water, and shall be unclean until the even. :9 And a man that is clean shall gather up the ashes of the heifer, and lay them up without the camp in a clean place, and it shall be kept for the congregation of the children of Israel for a water of sprinkling; it is a purification from sin. :10 And he that gathereth the ashes of the heifer shall wash his clothes, and be unclean until*

the even; *and it shall be unto the children of Israel, and unto the stranger that sojourneth among them, for a statute forever.*

For us today, it's difficult to follow how contact with the heifer's remains and ashes causes one to be "unclean" even after he would "wash his clothes in water, and bathe his flesh in water", yet later provides a "purification from sin". However, I'd expect that 2000 or 3000 years ago, when animal sacrifices were commonplace, these passages likely had very obvious and straightforward understandings to the people back then. The rabbi's answer was, yes, that is the case.

Now, everyone agrees that this section of Torah that we're now looking at (regarding "*thine that are dispersed be in the uttermost parts of heaven*") is referring to the times of Redemption and Moshiach (Messiah), so, it's clearly referring to some point in time from now to a point in the future. That being the case, together with the rabbi's answer, the plain literal meaning of the passage should be clear and obvious to us.

And it is!

The clear and obvious meaning for us is, "*If any of the exiles live in places like the Moon, Venus, Mars, or the moons of Jupiter and Saturn, even from those far-flung places God will gather them and return them to Israel.*" Those places are easily understood by us as the "ends of heaven", yet this is clearly in the context of the time of Redemption. This would seem to imply that the Redemption can be expected to come at a time when people can live in places in outer space. Well ... we don't have anyone living on the Moon or Mars now ... but we do have people living in the International Space Station – not many and not for very long times, but they do live there.

Now, we can return to our original passage, and we can see that Moshe is using the expression "end of heaven" as *both* a reference to time *and* place. He is saying, "*Nothing like this has happened since Man was created, and nothing like it will happen again until the time of Redemption, when people will be redeemed even from the Ends of Heaven."* That's now clear enough.

But, what about *at* the time of Redemption, or after? Apparently Moshe is hinting that something like the Revelation at Sinai will, indeed, happen again at that time.

For example, if God again comes down onto a mountain top to appear before an entire nation, it wouldn't happen in isolation before an obscure people in an obscure place. Modern communications technology will ensure that wherever it occurs, the entire world will see it ... live! If that happens, it can easily explain how all Mankind will come to recognize God, as is foretold in prophecy (e.g., *ZECHARIA 14:9 And the Lord shall become King over all the earth; on that day shall the Lord be one, and His name one*). Isn't it interesting how that all hangs together?

Appendix-3

Why Was That Fruit Forbidden?

Here's a different take on the narrative in Genesis about Adam and Eve and the "forbidden fruit":

> *GEN. 2:16-17 And the LORD God commanded the man, saying: 'Of every tree of the garden thou mayest freely eat; but of the tree of the knowledge of good and evil, thou shalt not eat of it; for in the day that thou eatest thereof thou shalt surely die.'*

Man was commanded not to eat this particular fruit, so the question arises, "*Why would God not want for people to have knowledge of Good and Evil by eating from this tree? After all, God made Man to be an intelligent being, made in His own image, and having Free Will. How could Man fulfill that destiny without knowledge of Good and Evil?*"

My own personal view of the answer is, *God indeed wanted Man to acquire knowledge of Good and Evil, but He wanted them to do it by EXERCISING THEIR BRAINS, NOT THEIR STOMACHS.* And what does this mean?

Symbolically it means that people need to learn about morality by exercising their brains to study God's precepts of Torah, rather than by following the guidance provided by their bodies' physical needs and desires, embodied by their stomachs.

The history of the 20th century also illustrates the answer. During that century, there arose an empire which became the largest in the history of the world, in terms of control of real estate, and arguably among the most powerful in history. This was, of course, the Soviet empire. This empire was never conquered. It was attacked by another powerful empire,

Nazi Germany, and emerged victorious. Yet, it eventually disintegrated from within, and by the end of the century, it was no more.

Now, the Soviet Union was founded on the philosophical principles of Karl Marx and Friedrich Engels, socialism/communism. The foundation of this philosophy is *materialism*, the doctrine that there is no Divine control over the world, indeed, there is no God, and that economic and physical motivations alone determine all human destiny. Or, putting it simply, that which tends to provide material prosperity and fills the stomach is Good, and that which tends to impoverish or prevent filling the stomach is Evil.

So, there it was, a gigantic virtually all-powerful empire built on the foundation that morality is a function of satisfaction of the "needs of the stomach". And that empire eventually fell apart due to its own internal corruption, decay, incompetence and weakness of determination. (It's perhaps interesting to notice that the other empire, Nazi Germany, derived its morality from the doctrine that Good comes from dominance by the Master Race – i.e., genetics, reproduction, rather than the workings of the brain. This empire lasted only 12 years.) God gave the world a lesson in what happens *when a society determines its morality on satisfaction of material needs*, i.e., *it cannot endure*. Rather, the members of a society need to "exercise their brains", by learning moral law through study of God's law, or at least through spiritual or non-material considerations.

Just looking at the Soviet philosophy of socialism with the view that it's only concerned with economics, and not with spiritually based morality, why would one think that socialism could be intrinsically in conflict with Torah? After all, socialism has to do with an economic system, whereas Torah has to do with a moral system. Yes, there are some economic directives in Torah, such as:

LEV. 19:35-36 Ye shall do no unrighteousness in judgment, in meteyard, in weight, or in measure. Just balances, just weights, a just ephah, and a just hin, shall ye have ...

But these are certainly the exception, not the rule. Isn't socialism really unrelated to Torah?

Well, no. If we look at the thinking and motivations behind socialism, a very different picture will emerge. The propensity toward socialism starts with the concern which today we call *Income Inequality*. "**It's *NOT FAIR* that the wealthy fellow over there earns more and has more than me. After all, we're both people and have the same intrinsic moral worth in society.**" It should be pretty obvious that this attitude directly conflicts with the Tenth Commandment:

EXO. 20:17 Thou shalt not covet thy neighbor's house; thou shalt not covet thy neighbor's wife, nor his man-servant, nor his maid-servant, nor his ox, nor his donkey, nor any thing that is thy neighbor's

It's probably a natural human tendency for one to have envy or resentment toward someone else who has more than oneself, especially if there might be no obvious reason why it should be so. Torah tells us that it's critically important to combat that tendency in oneself, so important that it's one of the seminal Ten Commandments given at Mt. Sinai. Why should it be so important?

It's because if this Commandment is not followed, then other moral problems will virtually inevitably ensue. Specifically, if our less-wealthy person looks at the more-wealthy person and doesn't see or understand why that other person has more wealth, he can easily come to believe that the wealthy person gained his wealth through cheating or theft, and then he might voice this belief to others. Since he would presumably have no real evidence upon which to base this belief, other than the wealth or income disparity itself, then in voicing this belief, he would be transgressing the Ninth Commandment "*Thou shalt not bear false witness against thy neighbor.*"

At this point, he may well feel justified in finding some way of rectifying this, in his view, unjust situation, and if he can accumulate enough political power by joining with like-minded others, he might persuade society's leadership to enact a method of Income/Wealth Redistribution through taxation. Although taxation is recognized as a legitimate means for a government to extract wealth from citizens, it's only proper application for funding necessary operations of the government itself, such as national defense. If the government uses taxation to "redistribute" income or wealth from one set of citizens to another, that is actually theft perpetrated under the color of government authority. Now, we are violating the Eighth Commandment, "*Thou shalt not steal*". [It's true that in context, Torah is here specifically enjoining against stealing people, i.e., kidnapping. However, the general principle applies, since the prohibition against generic stealing is also one of the Seven Commandments of the Children of Noah, applicable to all humanity (derived by implication from various sources within Torah).]

We can see that the problems are beginning to compound. Next, if the wealthier people protest at having their wealth taken from them in this manner, the more numerous less-wealthy people can complain that the wealthy people are being selfish and unjust, and they could publicize these views. This would be an attempt to embarrass the wealthy people, to coerce them into cooperating with the redistribution scheme.

In various places in the Talmud, we are told that embarrassing someone in public is equivalent to murdering him. Now, we are faced with transgressing the Sixth Commandment "*Thou shalt not murder*". [Note: the Hebrew verb used here applies in contexts beyond just premeditated murder, such as for negligent homicide. A more accurate, if less elegant, translation would be "*Thou shalt not cause wrongful death*". But in situations where this wrongful death is caused deliberately, it's actual murder.]

We can also note that in the extreme socialist, i.e., communist countries, such as the late Soviet Union, North Korea, People's Republic of China and Cuba, resistance to this kind of taxation could be considered an "economic crime", subject to capital punishment. So from the Torah view, this is literal transgression of the Sixth Commandment.

In socialist societies, there is a great premium placed on "Unity." By this it is meant that the will of "The People" is supreme and all citizens need to conform to it. And the intent of that will is determined by the government. And since that will is supreme, no dissent can be tolerated. To make sure no such dissent is being fomented among the people, the government will commonly encourage children to disclose if their parents are doing forbidden things or expressing forbidden ideas. This is usually done through schools and youth groups, where the teachers or group leaders ingratiate themselves to the children and thereby gain the children's trust and confidence toward the end of getting them to inform on their parents. Now, we see transgression of the Fifth Commandment, "*Honor thy father and thy mother*".

Once this happens, the bonds of love and trust between parents and children are broken. In extreme cases, the government takes actual control over the children and removes them from the parents' households. Now, the institution of the family is, at best, distorted, and at worst, destroyed. If the family unit is thereby damaged, then there's no need for a Commandment like the Seventh, "*Thou shalt not commit adultery*", since there's precious little left to adulterate.

Finally, a hallmark of socialist societies is government sponsored atheism. After all, it's the government that determines the Will Of The People, and that will includes the determination of morality: good and bad, right and wrong. Therefore there is no need also to have a God to provide such guidance.

Indeed, it's very inconvenient to the government to have a God Who provides morality rules at variance from those of the government. That's why there's typically such persecution of Jewish and Christian religious institutions in socialist/communist countries. So, now the Commandments of "*I am the LORD thy God ... Thou shalt have no other gods before Me. ... Thou shalt not make unto thee a graven image, ... Thou shalt not take the name of the LORD thy God in vain ...*" all become irrelevant and unnecessary.

And, of course, if there is no God, then there is no meaningful concept of Holiness, and the Fourth Commandment "*Remember the Sabbath day, to keep it holy*" also goes by the wayside.

So now we can clearly see how socialism is antithetical to Torah. In building a socialist society, the people must necessarily, at least to a discernible degree, transgress the moral Leadership of God and His Torah. And we understand why socialism is the wrong way to go.

www.ingramcontent.com/pod-product-compliance
Lightning Source LLC
Chambersburg PA
CBHW021009090426
42738CB00007B/724